PEGASUS ENCYCLOPEDIA LIBRARY

Space
EARTH

Edited by: Pallabi B. Tomar, Hitesh Iplani
Managing editor: Tapasi De
Designed by: Vijesh Chahal, Anil Kumar, Rohit Kumar
Illustrated by: Suman S. Roy, Tanoy Choudhury
Colouring done by: Vinay Kumar, Kiran Kumari & Pradeep Kumar

CONTENTS

Introduction 3

Formation of the Earth 4

Evolution of life on Earth 6

Earth as a planet 8

Earth's size and shape 9

Composition and structure 11

Tectonic plates 14

Rotation and Orbit 15

Influence of the sun and the moon 17

Spheres of the Earth 19

Gravity of the Earth 23

Rocks of the Earth 24

Cycles on and within the Earth 27

Earth in culture 30

Test Your Memory 31

Index 32

Introduction

Earth is a small planet in the vastness of space. It is one of nine planets that travel through space around the sun. The sun is a star, one of the billions of stars that make up a galaxy called the Milky Way. The Milky Way along with many as 100 billion other galaxies make up the universe.

The planet Earth is only a tiny part of the universe, but it is the home of human beings and in fact, all known life in the universe. Animals, plants and other organisms live almost everywhere on the Earth's surface. They can live on Earth because it is just the right distance from the sun. Most living things need the sun's warmth and light for life. If the Earth had been too close to the sun, it would have been too hot for living things. If the Earth had been too far from the sun, it would have been too cold for anything to survive . Living things also must have water to live. Earth has plenty. Water covers most of the Earth's surface.

> The study of Earth is called geology and the scientists who study Earth are geologists.

EARTH

Formation of the Earth

The Earth was formed approximately 4.6 billion years ago. The exact details of the formation of Earth are not known, but scientists have been able to develop a theory describing the events. Radioisotopic dating has aided scientists in forming theories that depict the formation of Earth.

It is beleived that the Earth was formed along with our solar system from a large cloud of spinning gas and dust. The spinning cloud of gas and dust eventually began to shrink due to gravity. As this happened, it slowly formed into a flatted disk rotating around a central core, which eventually became our sun. Over time, particles that were present in the dust cloud began to stick together and eventually formed planetesimals. A planetesimal is an object formed from dust, rock and other materials. Planetesimals can be anywhere in size from several metres to hundreds of kilometres. The term refers to small celestial bodies formed during the creation of planets. Larger planetesimals were able to attract smaller planetesimals due to their gravitational pull. Over time, planetesimals collided with one another due to gravity, which resulted in the formation of the planets in our solar system.

Astonishing fact

From a distance, Earth would be the brightest of the 9 planets. This is because sunlight is reflected on the planet's water!

Formation of the Earth

> **Geodesy is the branch of applied mathematics concerned with measuring or determining the shape of the Earth, its gravitational field and the location of fixed points.**

In the very beginning of Earth's history, this planet was a giant, red hot, boiling sea of molten rock—a magma ocean. The heat had been generated by the repeated high speed collisions of much smaller bodies of space rocks that continually clumped together as they collided to form this planet. As the collisions tapered off, the Earth began to cool, forming a thin crust on its surface. As the cooling continued, water vapour began to escape and condense in the Earth's early atmosphere. Clouds formed and storms raged, raining more and more water down on the primitive Earth, cooling the surface further until it was flooded with water, forming the seas.

It is theorized that the true age of the Earth is about 4.6 billion years, formed at about the same time as the rest of our solar system. The oldest rocks geologists have been able to find are 3.9 billion years old!

5

Evolution of life on Earth

After the formation of the planet Earth, it could not support life, for about a quarter of age. About billion years ago, our planet condensed to form a swirling cloud of interstellar dust and gas. The surface was too hot to allow the existence of protoplasm (the stuff of living cells). Even

> One-tenth of the Earth's surface is always under ice. And almost 90 per cent of that ice is to be found in the continent of Antarctica.

water, a major component of protoplasm was present only as vapour, one among many other gases in the hot, murky atmosphere.

About 3.5 million years ago life first began in water. Life arose from the non-living organic matter dissolved or suspended in water. All living objects originated from non-living material. The development of photosynthesis allowed the sun's energy to be harvested directly by life forms. The resultant oxygen accumulated in the atmosphere and formed a layer of ozone (a form of molecular oxygen [O3]) in the upper atmosphere. The incorporation of smaller cells within larger ones resulted in the development of complex cells called **eukaryotes**. True multicellular organisms formed as cells within colonies became increasingly specialized. Aided by the absorption of harmful ultraviolet radiation by the ozone layer, life was established on the surface of the Earth.

Evolution of life on Earth

Scientists have studied rocks using radiometric dating methods to determine the age of Earth. Another really helpful thing they have found in rocks which tell us more about the story of Earth's past are the remains of living creatures that have been embedded in the rocks since many ages. We call these fossils. It has been the careful study of Earth's fossil record that has revealed the exciting picture about the kinds of creatures that once roamed this planet. Fossilized skeletons of enormous creatures with huge claws and teeth, ancient ancestors of modern day species (such as sharks) that have remained virtually unchanged for millions of years and prehistoric jungles lush with plant life, all point to a abundance of life and a variety of species that continues to populate the Earth, even in the face of periodic mass extinctions.

Fossil of archaeopteryx

Human being constituted the pinnacle of evolution of life forms. Human beings have been on Earth for some 2 million years which is less than 1/1000 of the time for which life existed on Earth. Human beings are highly evolved species endowed with intelligence far superior to that of any other organism.

Astonishing fact

Worldwide, each day, 400 billion gallons (1,514,164,712,000 litres) of water is used!

EARTH

Earth as a planet

Earth ranks fifth in size among the nine planets. It has a diameter of about 13,000 km. Jupiter, the largest planet, is about 11 times larger in diameter than Earth. Pluto, (now called the 'dwarf planet') has a diameter less than one-fifth that of the Earth.

Earth, like all the planets in our solar system, travels around the sun in a path called an **orbit**. Earth is about 150 million km away from the sun. It takes one year for the Earth to complete one orbit around the sun. The innermost planet, Mercury, is only about one-third as far from the sun as the Earth and circles the sun in only 88 days. Pluto, is 40 times as far from the sun as the Earth and takes 248 Earth years to circle the sun!

Astonishing fact

Approximately 70 per cent of the Earth's surface is covered by water, but unfortunately 97 per cent of this water is saline which is present in the various oceans of the world and hence of no use.

Earth as a planet

Earth's size and shape

Earth's size

As the largest of the terrestrial planets, Earth has an estimated mass of 5.9736×1024 kg. Its volume is also the largest of the planets at $108.321 \times 1010 km^3$.

In addition, Earth is the densest of the terrestrial planets as it is made up of a crust, mantle and core. The Earth's crust is the thinnest of these layers while the mantle comprises 84 per cent of Earth's volume and extends 2,900 km below the surface. What makes Earth the densest of these planets however is its core. Earth's average density is 5515×10 kg/m^3. Mars, the smallest of the terrestrial planets by density, is only around 70 per cent as dense as the Earth.

Earth is classified as the largest of the terrestrial planets based on its circumference and diameter as well. At the equator, Earth's circumference is 40,075.16 km. It is slightly less between the North and South poles at 40,008 km. Earth's diameter at the poles is 12,713.5 km while it is 12,756.1 km at the equator. For comparison, the largest planet in Earth's solar system, Jupiter has a diameter of 142,984 km.

The distance from the surface of Earth to its centre is about 6,378 km.

Earth's shape

Earth's circumference and diameter differ because its shape is classified as an oblate spheroid or ellipsoid, instead of a sphere. This means that instead of being of equal circumference in all areas, the poles are squished, resulting in a bulge at the equator, and thus a larger circumference and diameter there.

The equatorial bulge at the Earth's equator is measured at 42.72 km and is caused by the planet's rotation and gravity. Gravity itself causes planets and other celestial bodies to contract and form a sphere. This is because it pulls all the mass of an object as close to the centre of gravity (the Earth's core in this case) as possible.

As the Earth rotates, this sphere is distorted by the centrifugal force. This is the force that causes objects to move outward away from the centre of gravity. Therefore, as the Earth rotates, centrifugal force is greatest at the equator so it causes a slight outward bulge there, giving that region a larger circumference and diameter.

Astonishing fact

The lowest point on the Earth's surface exists in the Dead Sea in the Middle East which is about 400 m below sea level.

Composition and structure

Earth's interior structure includes the crust, mantle, inner core and outer core. The crust and mantle are rocky. The inner and outer cores are metallic.

People often think of the planet Earth as being mostly made by water because most of Earth's surface is covered by water. However, the interior composition and structure of the Earth is quite different from its surface. Earth's interior is mostly rocky or metallic and is layered into the crust, mantle, inner core and outer core with the denser metallic materials concentrated towards the centre.

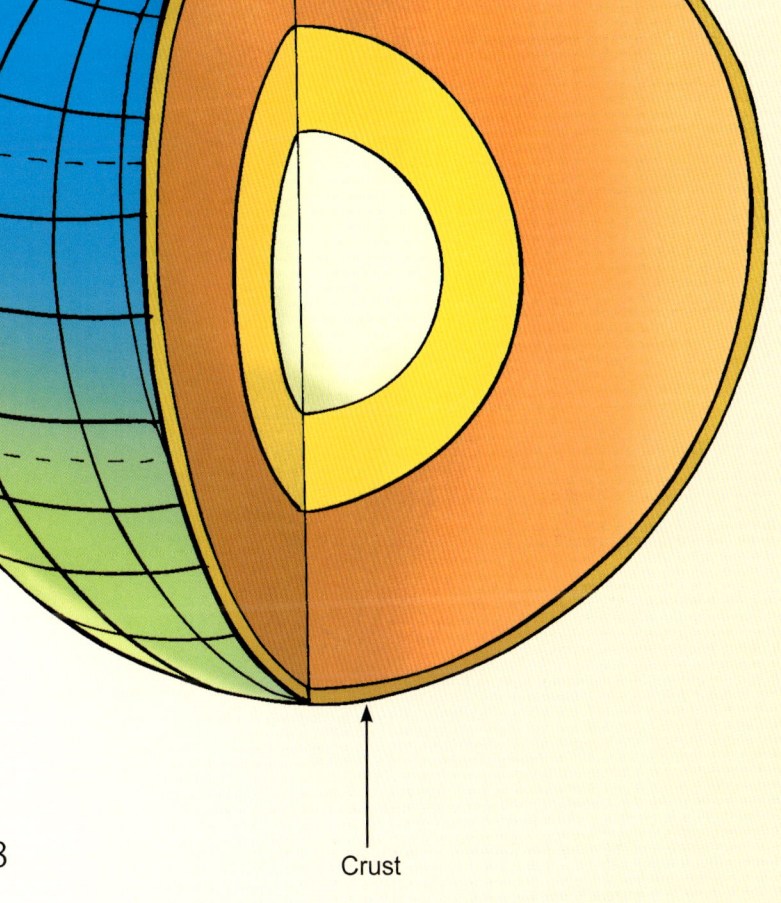

Crust

Earth's crust

The crust is the Earth's outermost layer, and it is the only layer that scientists can directly study. Earth's crust ranges from 8 to 70 km thick. It is solid and has a rocky composition. The top portion of the crust is the only portion of Earth's interior that geologists can study directly.

The crust is divided into tectonic plates that float on the mantle. The slow drifting of these tectonic plates causes most of the Earth's geological processes.

Astonishing fact

The temperature of Earth near the centre is thought to be at least 3,870 degree Celsius!

Earth's mantle

Like the crust, Earth's mantle has a rocky composition. Most people would describe the rocky mantle as being solid, however technically it is not really solid. The mantle is in a semi-solid state that can flow very slowly.

Heat sources in the core cause convection currents in the slowly flowing mantle. These convection currents cause the continental plates in Earth's crust to drift and transfer heat energy from Earth's core to the upper mantle and crust.

Earth's mantle is about 2900 km thick.

Astonishing fact

Other planets and moons in our solar system have volcanoes, but they do not have mountain ranges like the Earth because only Earth has plate tectonics.

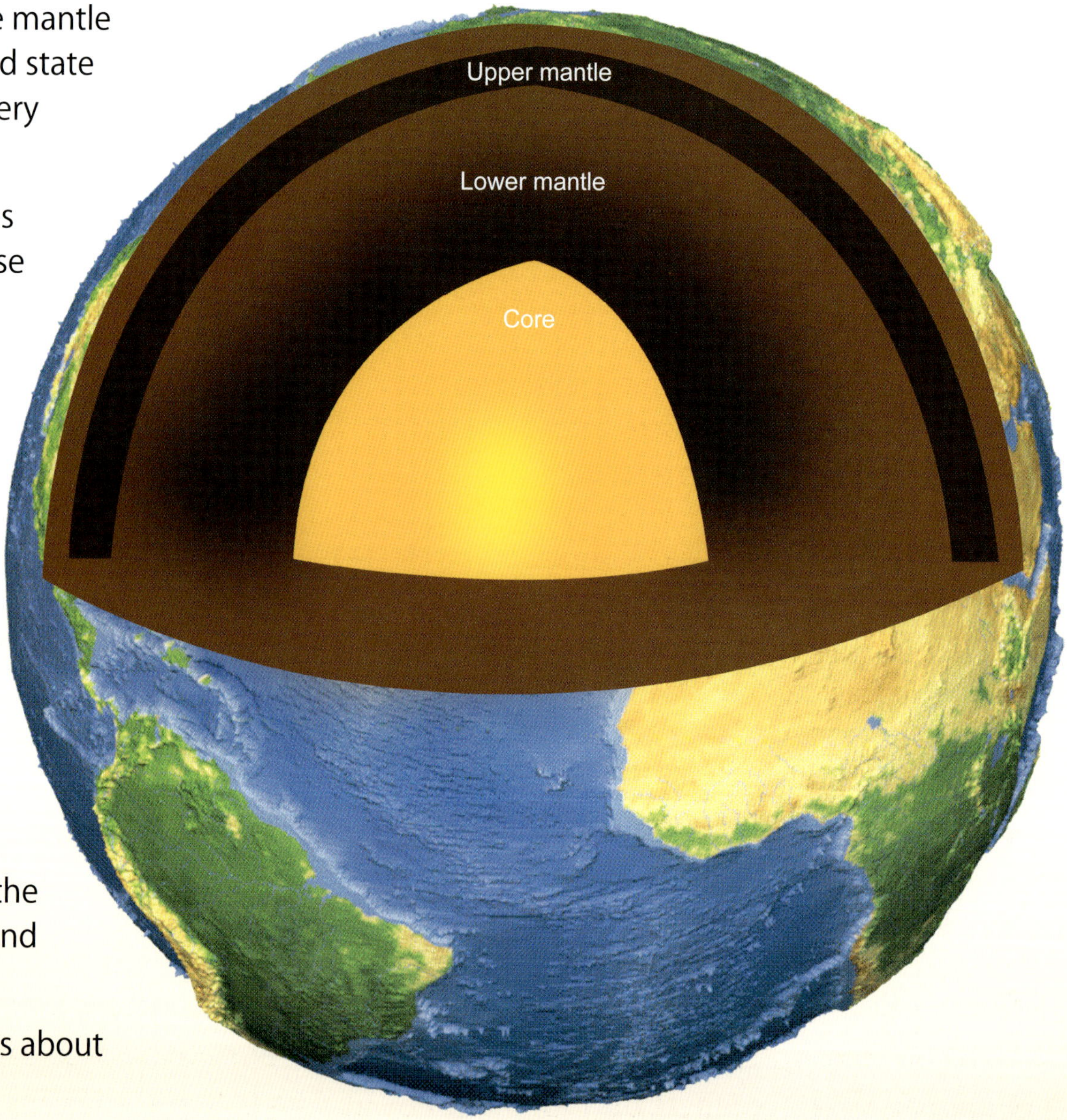

Composition and structure

Astonishing fact

Most of the Earth's deserts are not composed entirely of sand. About 85 per cent of them are rocks and gravel.

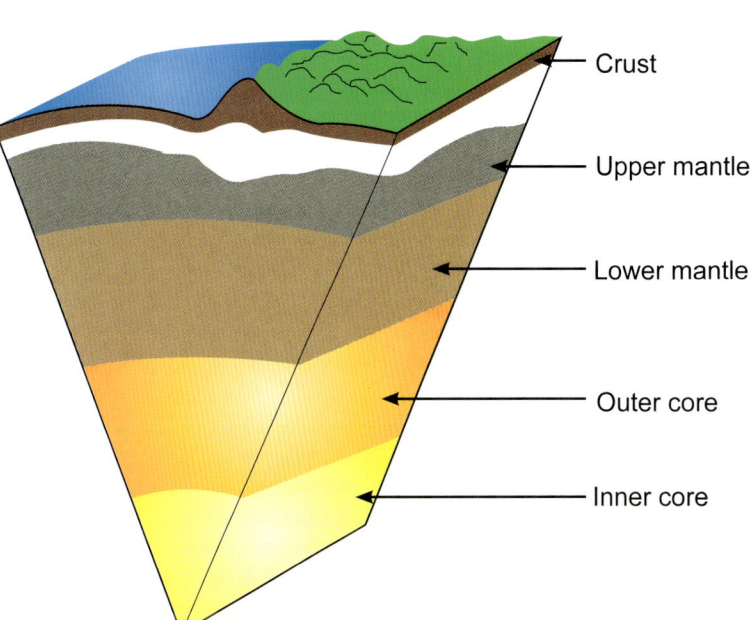

Earth's core

The inner part of the Earth is the **core**. This part of the Earth is about 2,900 km below the Earth's surface. The core is a dense ball of the elements iron and nickel. It is divided into two layers, the inner core and the outer core. The inner core or the centre of the Earth is solid and about 1,250 km thick. The outer core is so hot that the metal is always molten, but the inner core pressures are so great that it cannot melt, even though temperatures there reach 3700 degrees Celsius. The outer core is about 2,200 km thick. As the Earth rotates, the outer core spins around the inner core and that causes the Earth's magnetism.

Astonishing fact

Pangaea or the undivided landmass was not the beginning position of the land on Earth, but one of the six lost worlds that have come and gone. Pangaea was preceded by Pannotia about 550-650 million years ago and by Rhodinia around 1.8 billion years ago. Before them, at intervals of roughly 500 million years, Nuna, Kenorland, and Ur existed and then broke up.

13

Tectonic plates

Tectonic plates are large plates of rock that make up the foundation of the Earth's crust and the shape of the continents. The tectonic plates comprise the bottom of the crust and the top of the Earth's mantle. There are ten major plates on the Earth and many more minor ones. They float on a plastic-like part of the Earth's mantle called the **asthenosphere**. The plates are most famously known for being the source of earthquakes. When plates push up against each other, they create mountain ranges and volcanoes. Mt. Everest was created in this manner.

With time, plate tectonics has caused the world's continents to be reshaped. Every continent on Earth was once a part of an ancient supercontinent known as Pangaea, and Antarctica was once located in a temperate climate. Marine fossils can be found on the peaks of the world's tallest mountains. The tectonic plates continue to move slowly, but it is unlikely that their movement will cause the world's face to change more rapidly than the growing technological influence of mankind.

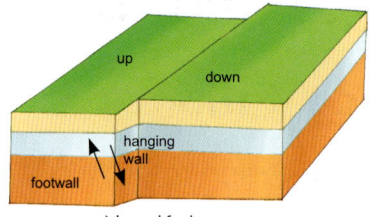
Normal fault

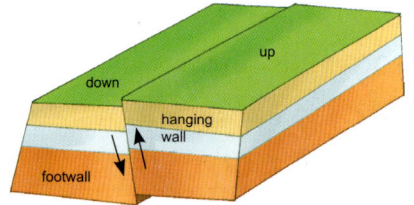
Reverse fault

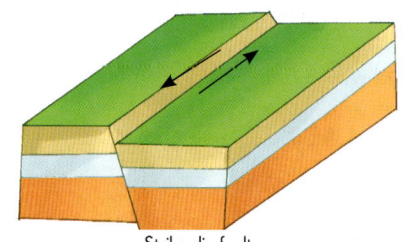
Strike-slip fault

Astonishing fact

Plate tectonics contributed to making Earth habitable by creating volcanoes. The water vapour and other gases emitted by volcanoes during Earth's early years helped to create Earth's oceans and atmosphere.

Rotation and Orbit

The Earth's rotation

The term Earth's rotation refers to the spinning of our planet on its axis. If the Earth is viewed from the North Pole from space, you will notice that the direction of rotation is counter-clockwise. The opposite is true if the Earth is viewed from the South Pole. One rotation takes twenty-four hours and is called a **mean solar day**.

The Earth is constantly rotating around an axis (called its rotational axis). Some objects rotate about a horizontal axis, like a rolling log. Some objects, such as a skater, rotate about a vertical axis. The Earth's axis is tipped over about 23.5 degree from vertical.

The Earth rotates around once in 24 hours—a rate of 1609 km per hour! The time it takes for the Earth to rotate completely around once is what we call a day. The Earth's rotation is responsible for the daily cycles of day and night. At any one moment in time, one half of the Earth is in sunlight, while the other half is in darkness. The Earth's rotation also creates the apparent movement of the sun across the horizon.

The combined effect of the Earth's tilt and its motion on its orbital path results in seasons.

> The amount of carbon dioxide in water and atmosphere and the amount of solar energy the planet receives are two factors that control the future of life on Earth and the planet itself.

EARTH

Orbit of Earth

The Earth's orbit is the motion of the Earth around the sun at an average distance of about 150 million km. Earth's travels around the sun on an elliptical orbit. This means there are times when the Earth is closer and times that it's further from the sun.

The closest point of this elliptical orbit is called the **perihelion**. At this point, the Earth is only 147 million km from the sun.

At its furthest point, which astronomers call **aphelion**, Earth is 152 million km.

There's a significant difference between these two points. And this can actually vary the amount of sunlight that reaches our planet. The perihelion happens in January when the northern hemisphere is tilted away from the sun experiencing winter. The southern hemisphere is tilted towards the sun experiencing summer. Earth takes 365.256 days to complete one orbit around the sun.

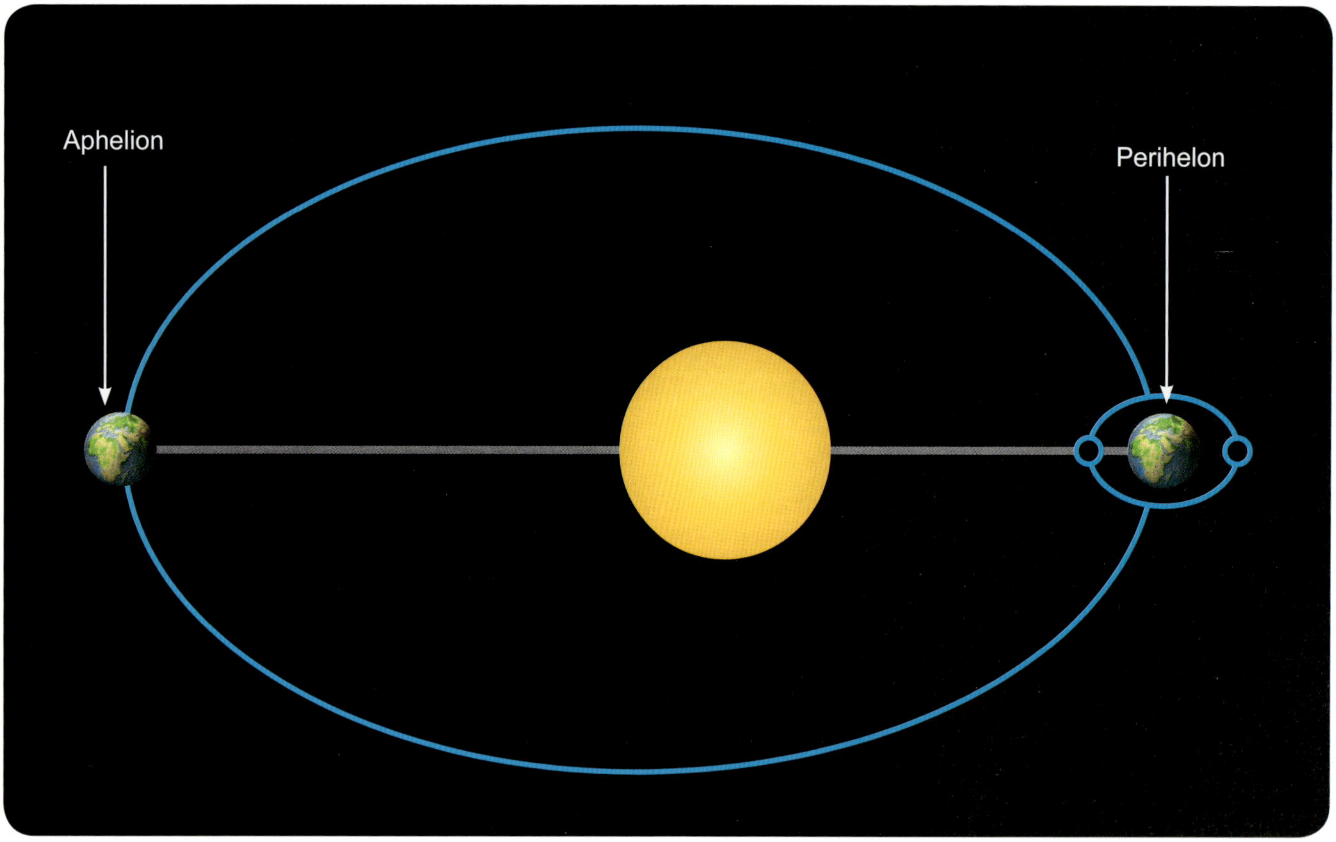

Aphelion — Perihelon

Astonishing fact

Earth, which can be viewed as a metal ball coated with rock, hurtles through space at 107,000 km per hour!

Influence of the sun and the moon

The moon orbits the Earth and in turn, the Earth orbits the sun. We see the universe from a platform that is both rotating on its axis, and travelling in an elliptical orbit around the sun. The Earth's rotation on its axis makes the sun rise in the east and set in the west. It is also a big part of why the moon rises and sets too; although, the moon takes 29 days to complete an orbit around the Earth as well.

The average distance from the Earth to the moon is 384,403 km and the average distance from the Earth to the sun is 149,597,887 km. If you divide these two numbers, you get approximately 389. Now, if you divide the diameter of the sun (1.4 million km) by the diameter of the moon (3,474 km), you get 403. Those two numbers are pretty close. This is why the moon and the sun appears to be the same size in the sky.

Astonishing fact

The birth of Earth's moon is extremely important because it stabilizes the Earth's tilt. Without the moon, Earth would have wild changes in the climate and be uninhabitable. The stabilizing tug of the moon tempers Earth, resulting in the minor tip that causes seasons.

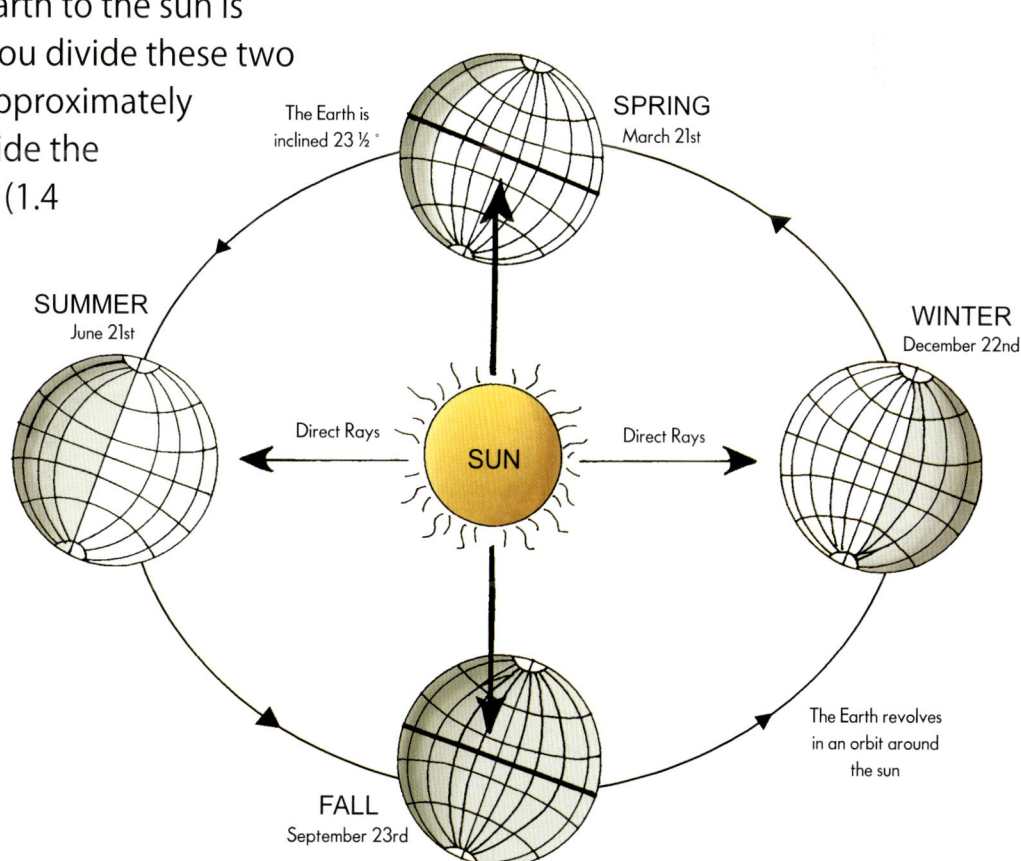

EARTH

As they appear to be the same size in the sky, the sun, Earth and the moon work together to create eclipses. When the moon is directly in between the Earth and sun, we see a solar eclipse. The moon appears to pass in front of the sun and darken it completely. And in the opposite situation, when the Earth is in between the sun and the moon, the Earth's shadow darkens the moon. This is a lunar eclipse. We don't see eclipses every month because the moon's orbit is tilted slightly away from the Earth's orbit around the sun. Sometimes the moon is above this orbit and sometimes it's below, so it doesn't block the light from the sun, or get caught in the Earth's shadow.

The sun and the moon work together to create the tides we experience here on Earth. Most of the rise in the tides comes from the gravitational pull of the moon, but a small amount comes from the sun.

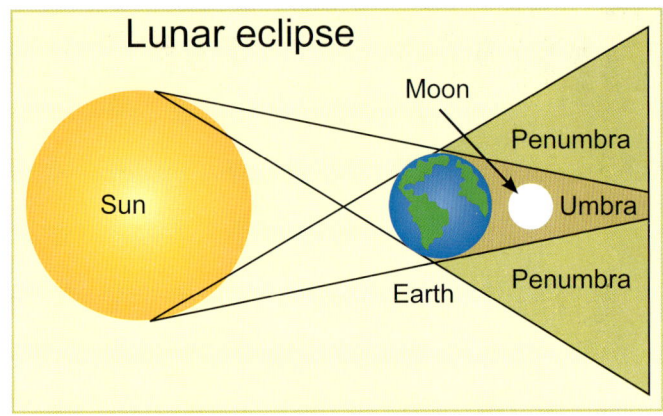

When the two heavenly bodies are on the same side of the Earth, we get the highest and the lowest tides, and when they are on opposite sides of the Earth, the tides are less extreme.

The brightest object in the sky is the sun and all of the moon's brightness is just the reflected light from the sun.

Astonishing fact

One of the driest places on the planet, Antarctica receives precipitation in the form of rain or snowfall only about once or twice a year.

Spheres of the Earth

Earth is composed of several layers, or spheres, somewhat like the layers of an onion. The solid Earth consists of a thin outer layer, the crust, with a thick rocky layer, the mantle, beneath it. The crust and the upper portion of the mantle are called the **lithosphere**. At the centre of the Earth is the core. The outer part of the core is liquid, while the inner part is solid. Much of the Earth is covered by a layer of water or ice called the **hydrosphere**. Earth is surrounded by a thin layer of air, the **atmosphere**. The portion of the hydrosphere, atmosphere, and solid land where life exists is called the **biosphere**.

Atmosphere

The atmosphere contains all the air in the Earth's system. It extends from less than 1 m below the planet's surface to more than 10,000 km above the planet's surface. The upper portion of the atmosphere protects the organisms of the biosphere from the sun's ultraviolet radiation. It also traps heat. When air temperatures in the lower portion of this sphere changes, weather occurs. As air in the lower atmosphere is heated or cooled, it moves around the planet. The result can be as simple as a breeze or as complex as a tornado.

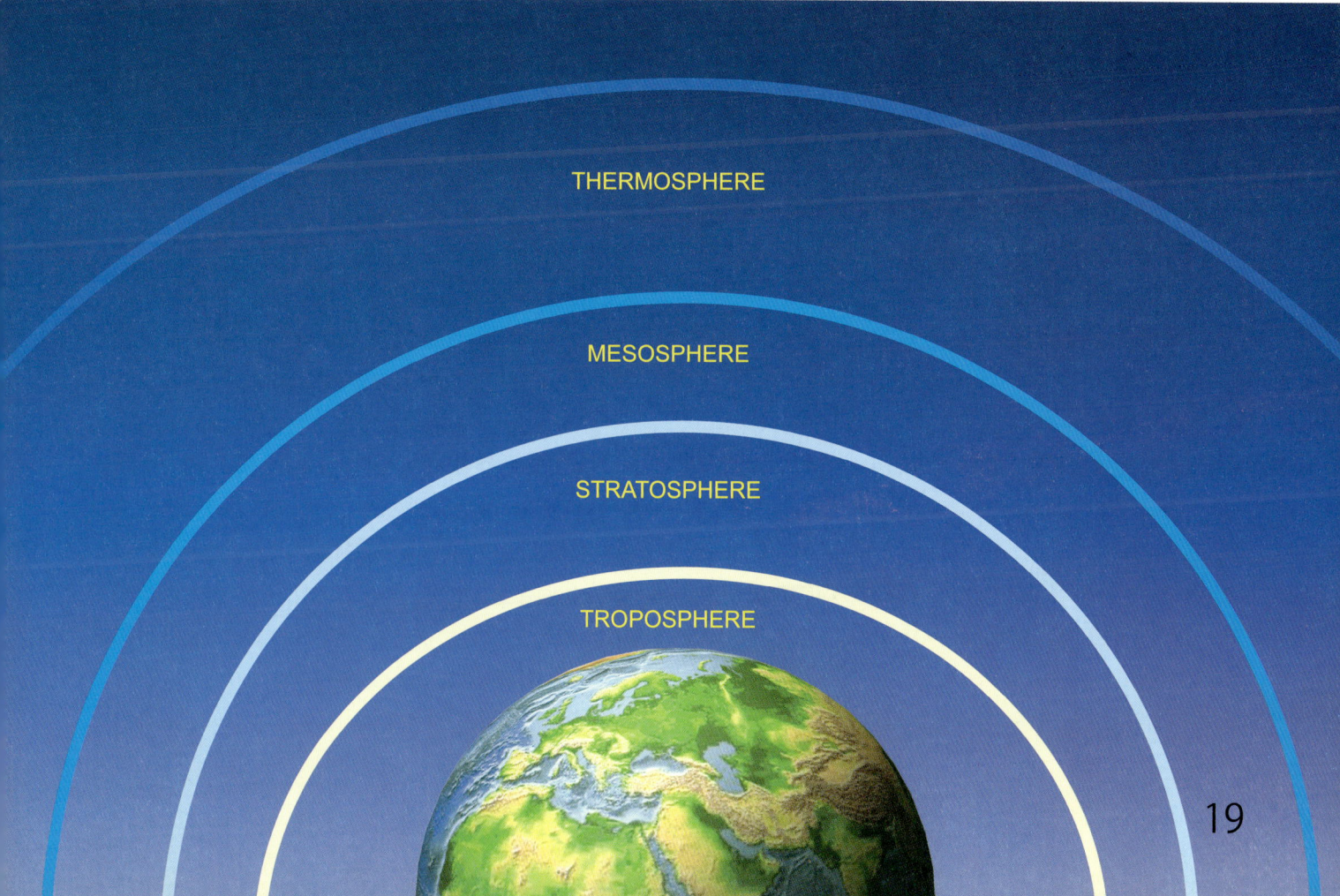

Astonishing fact

Although Earth's plates are made of solid rock, they buckle and twist like slabs of warm clay when they collide.

Hydrosphere

Earth is the only planet in the solar system with abundant liquid water on its surface. Water has chemical and physical properties not matched by any other substance, and it is essential for life on Earth. Water has a great ability to absorb heat. The oceans store much of the heat Earth gets from the sun. The electrical charges on water molecules give water a great ability to attract atoms from the other substances. This quality allows water to dissolve many things. Water's ability to dissolve materials makes it a powerful agent in breaking down rocks. Liquid water on Earth affects not just the surface but the interior as well. Water in the rocks lowers the melting temperature of rocks. Water dramatically weakens rocks and makes them easier to melt beneath Earth's surface.

About 71 per cent of Earth's surface is covered by water, most of it in the oceans. Ocean water is too salty to drink. Only about 3 per cent of Earth's water is fresh water, suitable for drinking. Much of Earth's fresh water is not readily available to people because it is frozen in the polar ice caps or beneath Earth's surface. Polar regions and high mountains stay cold enough for water to remain permanently frozen. The region of permanent ice on Earth is sometimes called the **cryosphere**.

Lithosphere

The lithosphere contains all of the cold, hard solid land of the planet's crust (surface), the semi-solid land underneath the crust, and the liquid land near the centre of the planet. The surface of the lithosphere is very uneven. There are high mountain ranges like the Rockies and Andes, huge plains or flat areas like those in Texas, Iowa, and Brazil and deep valleys along the ocean floor.

The solid, semi-solid, and liquid land of the lithosphere form layers that are physically and chemically different. If someone were to cut the Earth through its centre, these layers would be revealed like the layers of an onion. The outermost layer of the lithosphere consists of loose soil rich in nutrients, oxygen and silicon. Beneath that layer lies a very thin, solid crust of oxygen and silicon. Next is a thick, semi-solid mantle of oxygen, silicon, iron, and magnesium. Below that is a liquid outer core of nickel and iron. At the centre of Earth is a solid inner core of nickel and iron.

Astonishing fact

The sun's diameter is about 109 times greater than Earth's, whereas the Earth is just about four times larger in diameter than the moon.

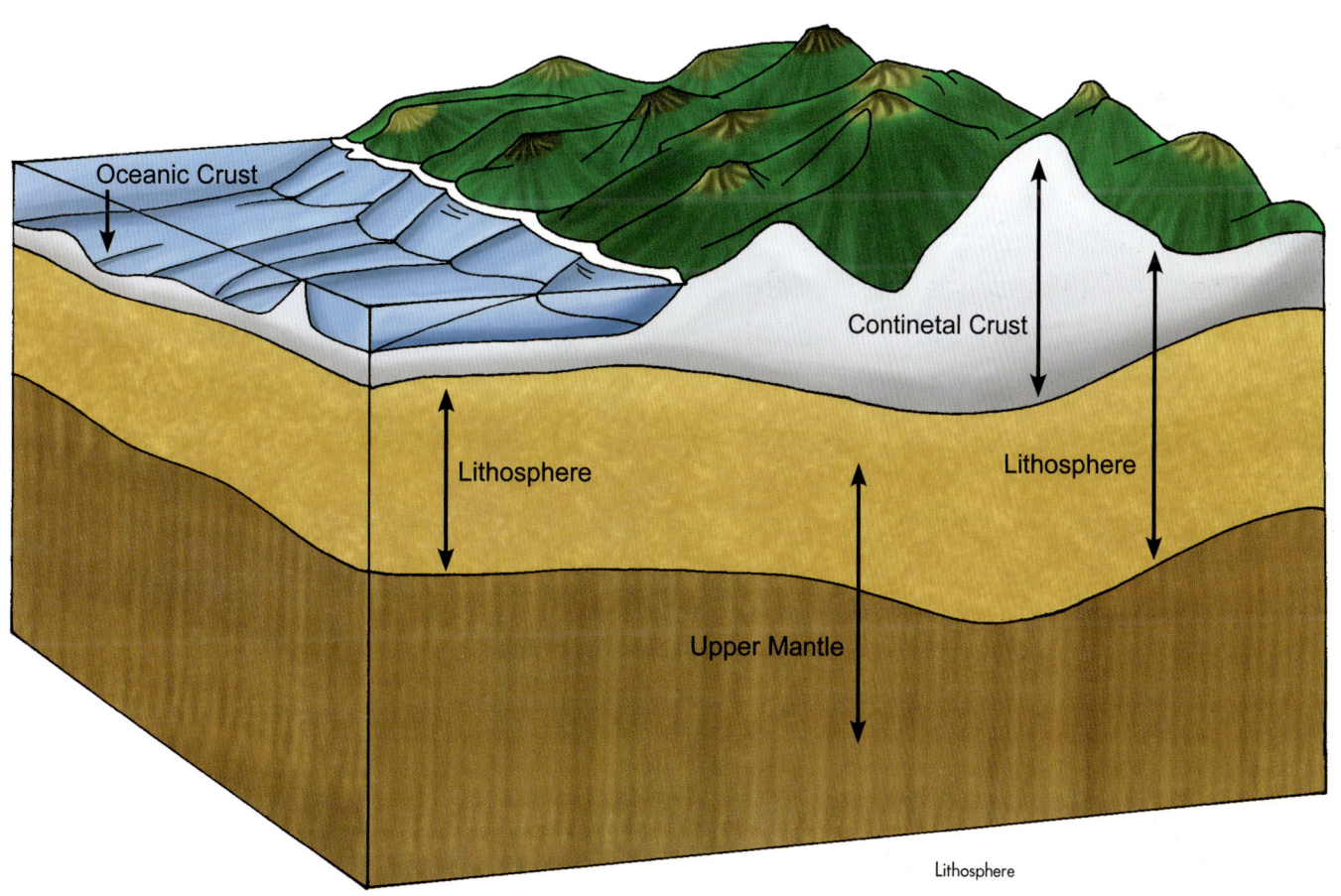

EARTH

Biosphere

The biosphere contains all the planet's living things. This sphere includes all of the microorganisms, plants and animals of Earth.

Within the biosphere, living things form ecological communities based on the physical surroundings of an area. These communities are referred to as biomes. Deserts, grasslands and tropical rainforests are three of the many types of biomes that exist within the biosphere.

Life affects Earth in many ways. Life has actually made the atmosphere around us. Plants take in water and carbon dioxide, both of which contain oxygen. They use the carbon in carbon dioxide and the hydrogen in water to make chemicals of many kinds and give off oxygen as a waste product. Animals eat plants to get energy and return water and carbon dioxide back into the environment.

Living things affect the surface of Earth in other ways as well. Plants create chemicals that speed the breakdown of rocks. Grasslands and forests slow the erosion of soil.

Astonishing fact

If you could evaporate all the water out of all the oceans and spread the resulting salt over all the land on Earth, you would have a 152 m layer coating everything.

Gravity of the Earth

Gravity causes the Earth to move around the sun. This phenomenon not only causes the Earth to keep moving around the sun, but also to keep the moon rotating around the Earth and it makes things fall to the ground. All matter, even the smallest object, has a gravitational force. The heavier the object, the stronger is its gravitational force.

The sun is far away but it's very heavy and has a big gravitational force with respect to the Earth. Due to the great speed, the Earth has the tendency to fly away from the sun. The gravity of the sun stops this, so that the Earth stays in its orbit. This also happens when you swing around an object on a rope. You feel the power by which you keep the item in its orbit as long as you keep swinging the rope. When you let it go, the item shoots outwards.

The Earth is also a big and heavy 'object' and also has a big gravity. This is why we keep staying on the ground and that everything you let go, falls to the ground. The moon spins around the Earth and keeps moving by the attraction of the Earth in the same way as the Earth keeps moving around the sun. But the moon also has its attraction to the Earth. We can see this every day on the beach when we witness the movements of high tide and low tide.

Astonishing fact

The 2.5 km thick ice sheet covering the continent of Antarctica constitutes around 90 per cent of the total fresh water. It is the largest store of fresh water on the planet.

Rocks of the Earth

The solid part of Earth consists of rocks, which are sometimes made up of a single mineral, but more often consist of mixtures of minerals. Geologists classify rocks according to their origin. Igneous rocks form when molten rock cools and solidifies. Sedimentary rocks form when grains of rock or dissolved chemicals are deposited in layers by wind, water or glaciers. Over time, the layers harden into solid rock. Metamorphic rocks develop deep in the Earth's crust when heat or pressure transforms other types of rock.

Igneous rocks

Igneous rocks form from molten material called **magma**. Most of Earth's interior is solid, not molten, but it is extremely hot. At the base of Earth's crust, the temperature is about 1000 degrees Celsius. In some portions of the crust, conditions are right for rocks to melt. Rocks can melt more easily near the crust if they contain water which lowers their melting point.

Rocks are like the Earth's blood because Earth's levels of air and water are kept in balance by the continuous circulation of rocks.

Rocks of the Earth

Astonishing fact
More than 80 per cent of the Earth's surface is made up of volcanic matter.

Sedimentary rocks

Sedimentary rocks make up about three-quarters of the rocks on the Earth's surface. They form at the surface in environments such as beaches, rivers, oceans and anywhere where sand, mud and other types of sediment collect. Sedimentary rocks preserve a record of the environments that existed when they formed. By looking at sedimentary rocks of different ages, scientists can figure out how climate and environments have changed through Earth's history. Fossils of ancient living things are preserved in sedimentary rocks too.

Many sedimentary rocks are made from the broken bits of other rocks. These are called **clastic** sedimentary rocks. The broken bits of rocks are called sediment. Sediment is the sand you find on the beach, the mud in a lake bottom, the pebbles in a river, and even the dust on furniture. The sediment may, in time, form a rock if the little pieces become cemented together.

There are other types of sedimentary rocks whose particles do not come from broken rock fragments. Chemical sedimentary rocks are made of mineral crystals such as halite and gypsum formed by chemical processes. The sediment particles of organic sedimentary rocks are the remains of living things such as clamshells, plankton skeletons, dinosaur bones and plants.

25

EARTH

Metamorphic rocks

When rocks are buried deeply, they become hot. Earth's crust grows hotter by about 25 degrees Celsius per km of depth. Pressure also increases with depth. As rocks are heated and subjected to pressure, minerals react and the rocks become metamorphic. Shale is transformed to slate, limestone eventually into marble under pressure.

Some rocks only change a little, while others change a lot. When a rock is metamorphosed, its mineral crystals change. Usually, the same chemical ingredients are used to form new crystals during metamorphism. Sometimes new types of minerals grow that weren't in the rock before.

The temperatures on the Earth range from -88 degree to 58 degree Celsius. 100 million years ago it was 6 to 12 degrees hotter than it is today. Alligators lived in what is now ice-covered Greenland.

Cycles on and within the Earth

Earth can be thought of as a huge system of interacting cycles. The cycles affect everything on the planet, from the weather to the shape of the landscape. There are many cycles on and within the Earth. A few of the most important are:

1. Atmospheric circulation
2. Ocean currents
3. The global heat conveyor
4. Hydrologic cycle
5. Rock cycle

Atmospheric circulation

The atmosphere, a thin blanket of gases that surrounds Earth, transports heat and water and filters out deadly ultraviolet radiation. Whether it is just a gentle breeze or a hurricane-force gale, Earth's atmosphere is constantly on the move.

When the atmosphere moves, it evens out differences in temperature between the chilly poles and the warm equator. Warm air from the equator moves toward the poles and cold air from the poles moves toward the equator. This circulation of air is disrupted a bit by the Earth's rotation. This makes counterclockwise winds around hurricanes, winter storms, tornadoes, and other low-pressure areas north of the equator and clockwise south of the equator.

Astonishing fact

The Pacific Ocean is one of the largest features on the face of the Earth, with an area of more than 181 million square km. It contains half of the world's water!

Ocean currents

Ocean currents are driven by the winds and follow the same general pattern. The continents block the flow of water around the globe, so ocean currents flow west near the equator, then turn toward the poles when they strike a continent, turn east, then flow back to the equator on the other side. In all the oceans, the ocean currents form great loops called **gyres**. The gyres flow clockwise north of the equator and counter clockwise south of it.

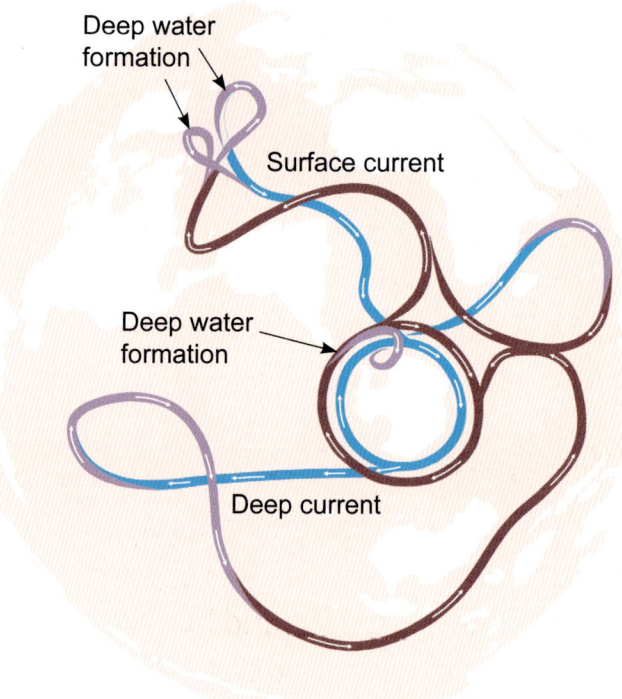

The global heat conveyor

The global heat conveyor

The global heat conveyor is an enormous cycle of ocean water that distributes the oceans heat around Earth. Water in the Polar regions is very cold, salty and dense. It sinks and flows along the sea floor toward the equator. Eventually, the water rises along the margins of the continents and merges with the surface water flow. When it reaches the Polar regions, it sinks again. This three-dimensional movement of water mixes heat throughout the oceans, warming polar waters. It also brings nutrients up from the deep ocean to the surface, where they are available for marine plants and animals.

> **It takes light 8 minutes 20 seconds to travel from the sun to the Earth.**

Cycles on and within the Earth

Hydrologic cycle

Water from the oceans evaporates and is carried by the atmosphere, eventually falling as rain or snow. Water that falls on the land helps break rocks down chemically, nourishes plants, and wears down the landscape. Eventually, the water returns to the sea to start the cycle over again.

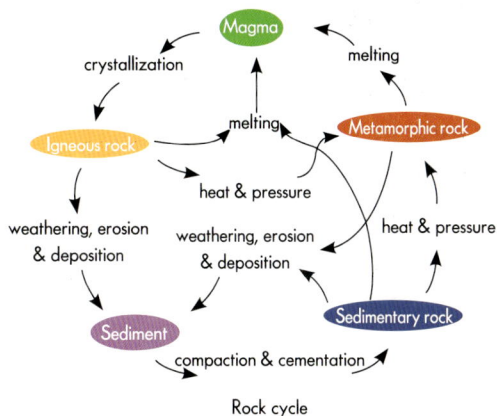

Rock cycle

Rock cycle

Earth has many kinds of rocks compared to other planets because there are so many processes acting to form and break down rocks. Geologists sometimes speak of the rock cycle to explain how different rock types are related. The cycle may begin with a flow of lava from a volcano cooling to form new igneous rocks on Earth's surface. As the rock is exposed to water, it breaks down and the resulting materials maybe carried away to be deposited as sedimentary rocks. These rocks may eventually be so deeply buried that they change in form to become metamorphic rocks. They may even melt, creating the raw material for the next generation of igneous rocks.

> **Astonishing fact**
> Earth doesn't take 24 hours to rotate on its axis. It's actually 23 hours, 56 minutes and 4 seconds.

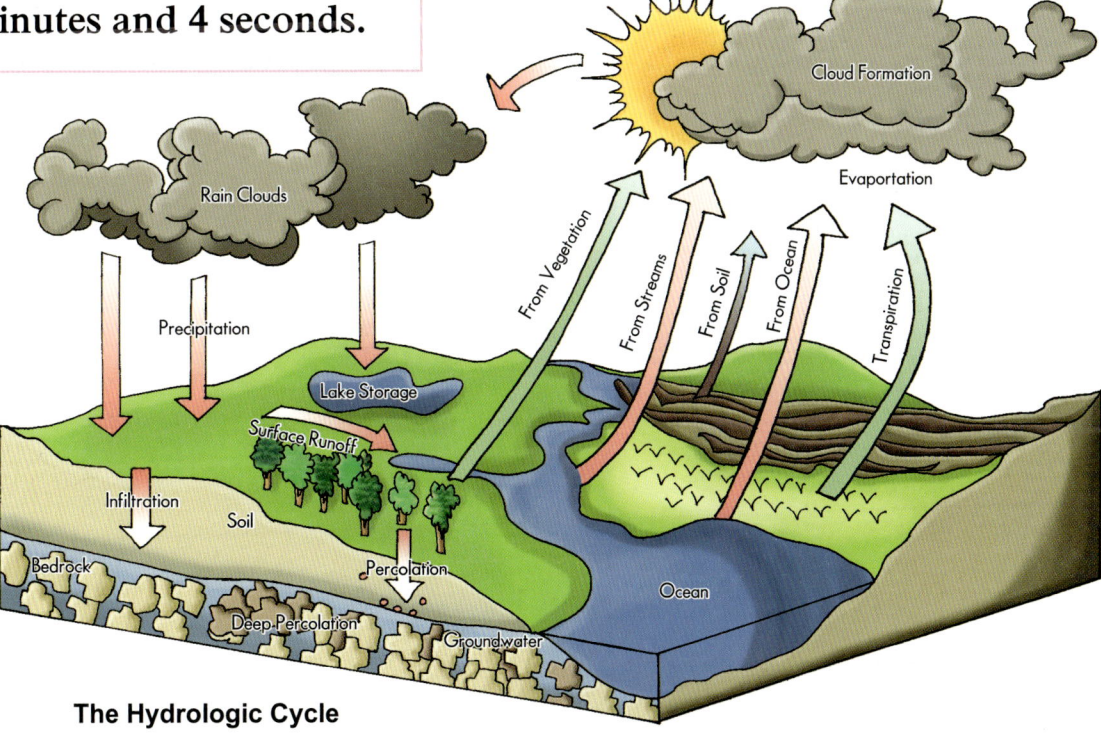

The Hydrologic Cycle

EARTH

Earth in culture

The name 'Earth' derives from the Anglo-Saxon word 'erda', which means 'ground or soil'. It is the only name for a planet of the solar system that does not come from Greco-Roman mythology. The standard astronomical symbol of the Earth consists of a cross circumscribed by a circle.

Unlike the rest of the planets in the Solar System, mankind did not recognize the Earth as a planet until the 16th century. Earth has often been personified as a deity, in particular a goddess. Creation myths in many religions recall a story involving the creation of the Earth by a supernatural deity or deities.

In the past there were varying levels of belief in a flat Earth, but this was displaced by the concept of a spherical Earth due to observation and circumnavigation. The human perspective regarding the Earth has changed following the advent of spaceflight and the biosphere is now widely viewed from a globally integrated perspective. This is reflected in a growing environmental movement that is concerned about mankind's effects on the planet.

Astonishing fact

A belief of some Native Americans was that the Earth is supported by a giant tortoise, which made the Earth tremble each time it took a step.

Test Your MEMORY

1. What is the Earth?

2. Write briefly about how the Earth was formed.

3. How did life evolve on Earth?

4. Write about the size and shape of the Earth?

5. What is the Earth composed of?

6. Write briefly about the orbit and rotation of the Earth?

7. Write what you know about the sun and the moon?

8. Describe briefly the spheres of the Earth.

9. Write about the gravitational force of Earth.

10. Write briefly about the Earth's rocks.

11. Write about the cycles on and in Earth.

12. How did the name Earth come into being?

Index

A
aphelion 16
asthenosphere 14
atmosphere 5, 6, 14, 15, 19, 22, 27, 29
atmospheric circulation 27

B
biosphere 19, 22, 30

C
celestial bodies 4, 10
centrifugal force 10
clastic 25
continents 14, 28
core 4, 9, 10, 11, 12, 13, 19, 21
crust 5, 9, 11, 12, 14, 19, 21, 24, 26
cryosphere 20

D
dating 4, 7

E
ellipsoid 10
elliptical orbit 16, 17
equator 9, 10, 27, 28
eukaryotes 6

G
galaxy 3
geologists 3, 5, 11, 24, 29

gravity 4, 10, 23
gyres 28

H
human being 7
hydrologic cycle 27, 29
hydrosphere 19

I
Igneous rocks 24
inner core 11, 13, 21
interstellar 6

J
Jupiter 8, 9

L
lithosphere 19, 21
lunar eclipse 18

M
magnetism 13
mantle 9, 11, 12, 14, 19, 21
Mercury 8
Metamorphic rocks 24, 26
Milky Way 3
Mt. Everest 14

N
northern hemisphere 16

O
oblate spheroid 10
ocean currents 27, 28

orbit 8, 16, 17, 18, 23
outer core 11, 13, 21

P
perihelion 16
planet 3, 6, 7, 8, 9, 10, 11, 15, 16, 18, 19, 20, 21, 22, 23, 27, 30
planetesimals 4
Pluto 8
protoplasm 6

R
radiation 6, 19, 27
rock cycle 27, 29

S
Sedimentary rocks 24, 25
solar eclipse 18
southern hemisphere 16
sphere 10, 19, 22
sun 3, 4, 6, 8, 15, 16, 17, 18, 19, 20, 21, 23, 28

T
terrestrial 9
The global heat conveyor 27, 28
tides 18

U
Universe 3, 17

PEGASUS ENCYCLOPEDIA LIBRARY

Space
MOON

Edited by: Pallabi B. Tomar, Hitesh Iplani
Managing editor: Tapasi De
Designed by: Vijesh Chahal, Anil Kumar, Rohit Kumar
Illustrated by: Suman S. Roy, Tanoy Choudhury
Colouring done by: Vinay Kumar, Kiran Kumari & Pradeep Kumar

CONTENTS

The silvery moon 3

Origin and evolution of the moon 5

Composition of the moon 7

The interior of the moon 8

Physical characteristics 11

Orbit 16

Relation with Earth 23

Study and exploration 25

Moon in mythology 29

Test Your Memory 31

Index 32

Astonishing fact

The oldest known map of the moon, about 5,000 years old was found carved into a rock in a prehistoric tomb at Knowth, County Meath, in Ireland.

The silvery moon

Moon is Earth's only natural satellite. It is the brightest object in the night sky but gives off no light of its own. Instead, it reflects light from the sun. Like the Earth and the rest of the solar system, the moon is about 4.6 billion years old.

The moon is a roughly spherical, rocky body orbiting the Earth at an average distance of 385,000 km. It measures about 3,475 km across, a little over one-quarter of Earth's diameter. Earth and the moon are the closest in size of any known planet and its satellite.

The moon has no life of any kind. Compared to the Earth, it has changed little over billions of years. On the moon, the sky is black even during the day and the stars are always visible.

MOON

The footprints left by Apollo astronauts will last for centuries because there is no wind on the moon. The moon does not possess any atmosphere, so there is no weather as we are used to on Earth. As there is no atmosphere to trap heat, the temperatures on the moon are extreme, ranging from 100 degree Celsius at noon to -173 degree Celsius at night!

The moon is covered with rocks, boulders, craters and a layer of charcoal-coloured soil from 1.5 to 6 m deep. The soil consists of rock fragments, pulverized rock and tiny pieces of glass. Two types of rock are found on the moon— **basalt**, which is hardened lava and **breccia**, which is soil and rock fragments that have melted together.

Astonishing fact

When Neil Armstrong took that historical step of 'one small step for man one giant step for mankind', it would not have occurred to anyone that the step he took in the dust of the moon was there to stay. It will be there for at least 10 million years!

The moon has no weather, no wind, rain or air. As a result, it has no protection from the sun's rays or meteorites and no ability to retain heat.

Origin and evolution of the moon

Scientists believe that the moon formed as a result of a collision known as the Giant Impact or the 'Big Whack.' According to this idea, Earth collided with a planet-sized object 4.6 billion years ago. As a result of the impact, a cloud of vaporized rock shot off Earth's surface and went into orbit around Earth. The cloud cooled and condensed into a ring of small, solid bodies, which then gathered together, forming the moon.

The rapid joining together of the small bodies released much energy as heat. Consequently, the moon melted, creating an 'ocean' of magma (melted rock).

The magma ocean slowly cooled and solidified. As it cooled, dense, iron-rich materials sank deep into the moon. Those materials also cooled and solidified, forming the mantle, the layer of rock beneath the crust.

Astonishing fact
Apollo 11 had only 20 seconds of fuel left when they landed on the moon!

MOON

The evolution of the moon has been completely different from that of the Earth. For about the first 700 million years of the moon's existence, it was struck by great numbers of meteorites. They blasted out craters of all sizes. The sheer impact of so many meteorites caused the moon's crust to melt. Eventually, as the crust cooled, lava from the interior surfaced and filled in cracks and some crater basins. These filled-in basins are the dark spots we see when we look at the moon.

Astonishing fact

In China, the dark shadows that are on the moon are called 'the toad in the moon'.

To early astronomers, these dark regions appeared to be bodies of liquid. In 1609, the Italian astronomer Galileo Galilei became the first person to observe the moon through a telescope. He named these dark patches 'maria,' Latin for 'seas.'

In 1645, the Polish astronomer Johannes Hevelius, known as the father of lunar topography, charted 250 craters and other formations on the moon. Many of these were later named for philosophers and scientists, such as Danish astronomer Tycho Brahe, Polish astronomer Nicolaus Copernicus, German astronomer Johannes Kepler and Greek philosopher Plato.

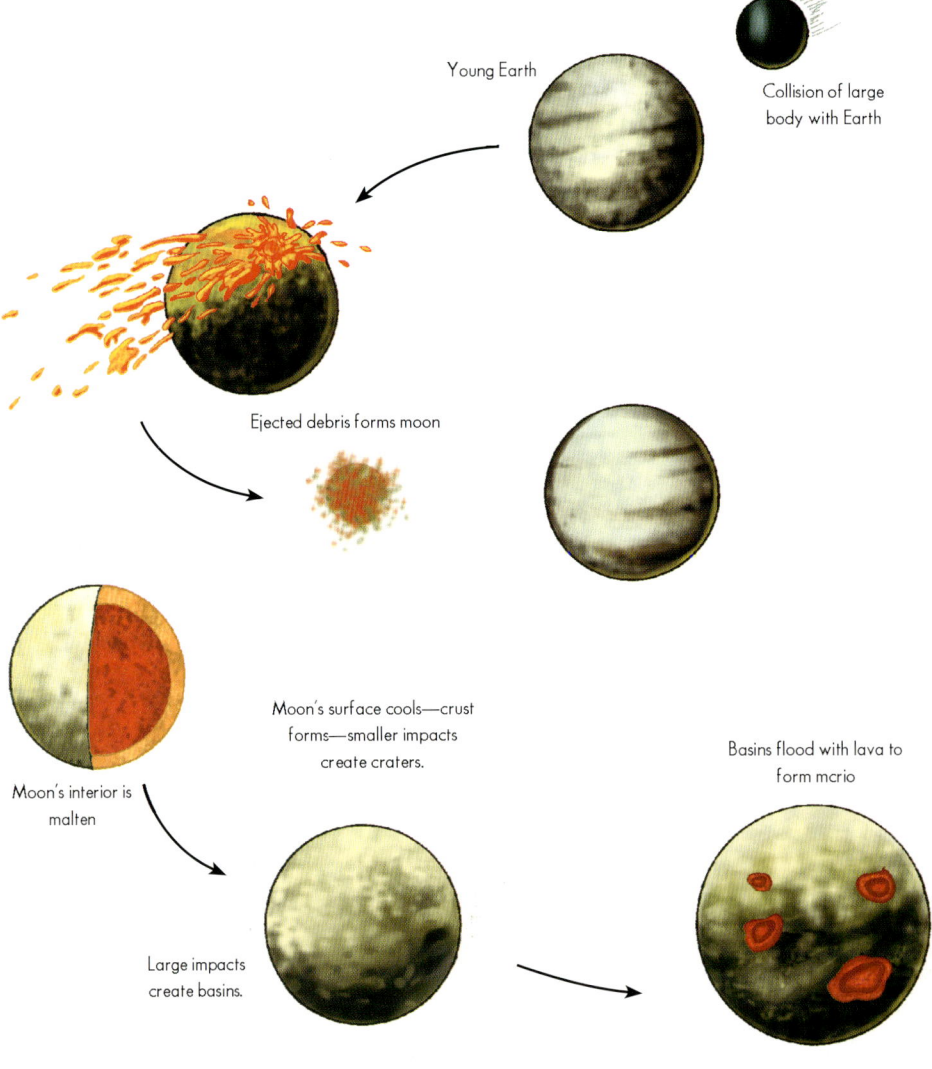

Young Earth

Collision of large body with Earth

Ejected debris forms moon

Moon's interior is molten

Large impacts create basins.

Moon's surface cools—crust forms—smaller impacts create craters.

Basins flood with lava to form mario

Birth of moon

6

Astonishing fact
The dark spots we see on the moon that create the image of the man in the moon are actually craters filled with basalt, which is a very dense material.

Composition of the moon

The moon's composition has been of great interest to scientists. With the collection of moon soil and moon rocks by astronauts, many questions have been answered. Moon soil contains no fossils of plants or animals, but when this soil is placed on Earth plants, they seem to grow better.

Moon rocks are composed of minerals including aluminum, calcium, magnesium, oxygen, silicon and titanium. Some gases are also trapped in these rocks, such as hydrogen and helium.

Astronauts collect two main types of rock, basalt and breccia. Basalt is formed from hardened lava and is made of feldspar, proxene and ilmenite crystals. These minerals were formed at 2200 degrees, which proves that the moon was extremely hot when it was forming. Breccia is made of soil and rock that have been squeezed together when hit by falling objects.

The interior of the moon

The moon, like the Earth, has three interior zones— crust, mantle and core. However, the composition, structure, and origin of the zones on the moon are much different from those on Earth.

Most of what scientists know about the interior of the moon has been learnt by studying moonquakes. The data on moonquakes come from scientific equipment set up by Apollo astronauts from 1969 to 1972.

Crust

The average thickness of the lunar crust is about 70 km, compared with about 10 km for Earth's crust. The outermost part of the moon's crust is broken, fractured and jumbled as a result of the large impacts it has endured. This shattered zone gives way to intact material below a depth of about 9 km. The bottom of the crust has an abrupt increase in rock density at a depth of about 60 km on the near side and about 80 km on the far side.

The moon's crust is composed of a dusty outer rock layer called a **regolith**. The term regolith refers to a rocky layer resembling concrete, which has been broken and blasted apart, then fused back together somehow. Like the Earth's crust, the moon's crust seems to contain some magnetism. Both the crust and regolith of the moon are unevenly distributed over the entire moon.

It takes about 1.25 seconds for moonlight to reach the Earth.

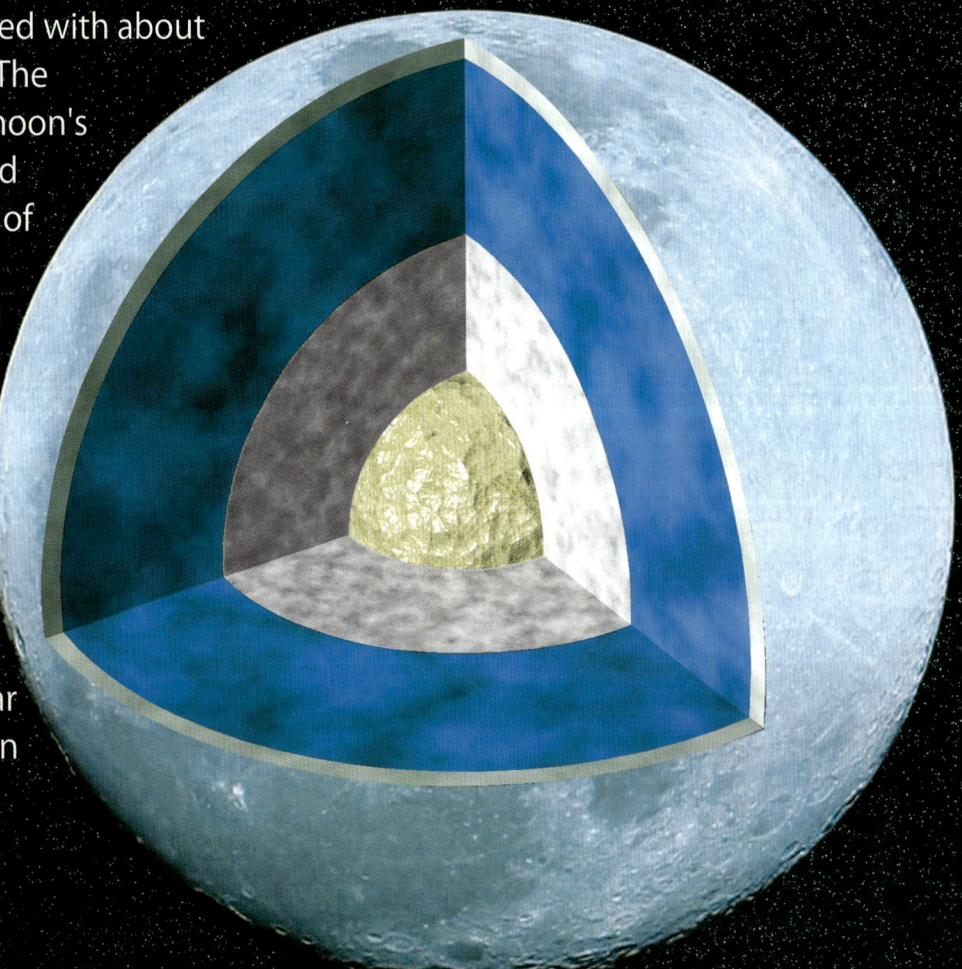

The interior of the moon

Mantle

The mantle of the moon consists of dense rocks that are rich in iron and magnesium. The mantle is formed during the period of global melting. Low-density minerals floated to the outer layers of the moon, while dense minerals sank deeper into it.

Later, the mantle partly melted due to heat building up in the deep interior. The source of the heat was probably the decay (breakup) of uranium and other radioactive elements. This melting produced basaltic magmas—bodies of molten rock. The magmas later made their way to the surface and erupted as mare lavas and ashes. Although, mare volcanism occurred for more than 1 billion years, much less than 1 per cent of the volume of the mantle ever remelted.

Astonishing fact

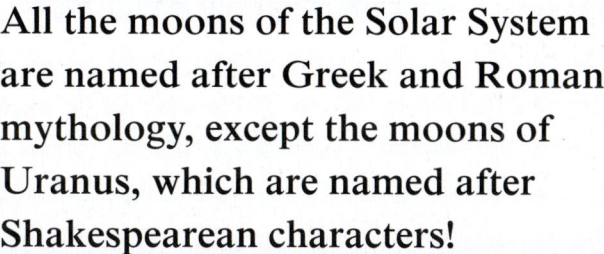

All the moons of the Solar System are named after Greek and Roman mythology, except the moons of Uranus, which are named after Shakespearean characters!

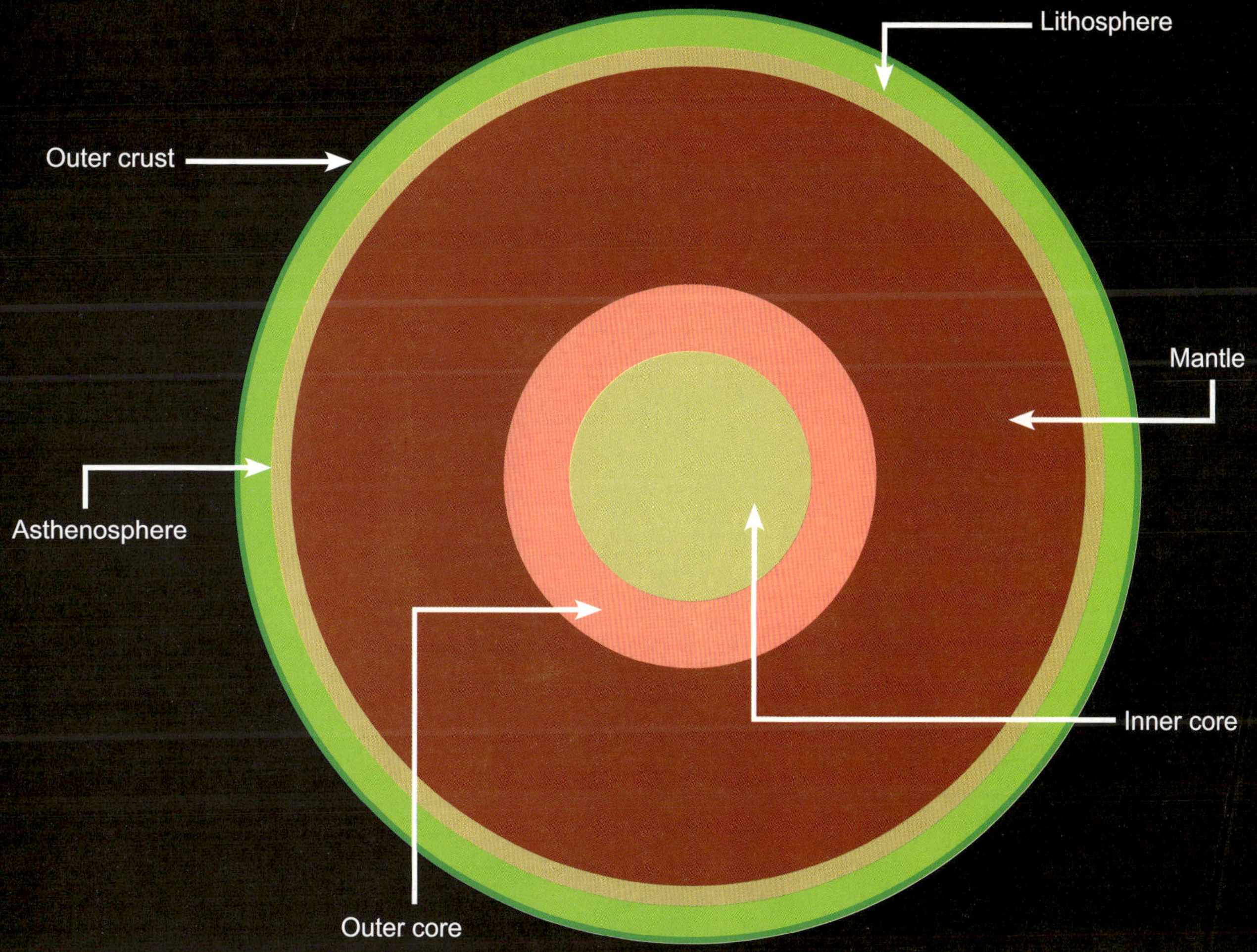

- Lithosphere
- Outer crust
- Asthenosphere
- Mantle
- Inner core
- Outer core

MOON

Jupiter's moon Ganymede is the largest moon in the Solar System and is larger than the planets Mercury and Pluto.

Libration

Libration is a rocking movement of the moon. Librations cause us to see the moon from different angles at different times, enabling us to see about 59 per cent of the moon's surface from Earth, even though the same side always faces us.

Shape of the moon

One important and beautiful phenomenon about the shape of the moon as it appears to the Earth is its 'waxing and waning'. The orbiting of the moon around the Earth and its own axis and the Earth's rotation around its axis causes this occurrence. Actually, no waxing and waning take place.

It is the illuminated portion of the moon that appears to the Earth make the people think so. The illuminated portion of the moon varies daily with the movement of the Earth, moon and the sun.

Physical characteristics

Mountains on the moon

There are several mountains and mountain ranges on the moon. Some of them are well over 3048 m tall. Most of the mountains on the moon are on the rims of large craters formed by meteorite impacts. The moon does not have jagged mountains; instead the moon's mountains are round and smooth.

Magnetic field

Compared to that of Earth, the moon has a very weak magnetic field. While some of the moon's magnetism is thought to be intrinsic, collision with other celestial bodies might have bestowed some of the moon's magnetic properties. Indeed, a long-standing question in planetary science is whether an airless solar system body, such as the moon, can obtain magnetism by the impact processes from comets and asteroids. Magnetic measurements can also supply information about the size and electrical conductivity of the lunar core — evidence that will help scientists better understand the moon's origins.

Astonishing fact

Moonquakes, which originate several miles below the moon's surface, maybe a result of the Earth's gravitational pull.

Orbit

The moon moves in a variety of ways. For example, it rotates on its axis, an imaginary line that connects its poles. The moon also orbits the Earth. Different amounts of the moon's lighted side become visible in phases because of the moon's orbit around Earth. During events called eclipses, the moon is positioned in line with Earth and the sun.

The Earth's moon is the fifth largest in the whole solar system, and is bigger than the planet Pluto. The moon has a nearly circular orbit which is tilted about 5 degree towards the plane of the Earth's orbit. Its average distance from the Earth is 384,400 km. The combination of the moon's size and its distance from the Earth causes the moon to appear the same size in the sky as the sun, which is one reason we can have total solar eclipses.

It takes the moon 27.322 days to go around the Earth once. Due to this motion, the moon appears to move about 13 degree against the stars each day, or about one-half degree per hour. If you watch the moon over the course of several hours one night, you will notice that its position among the stars will change by a few degrees. The changing position of the moon with respect to the sun leads to lunar phases.

> **Astonishing fact**
>
> The moon's gravity has slowed the speed of Earth's rotation. Long ago, it was much faster and days were much shorter.

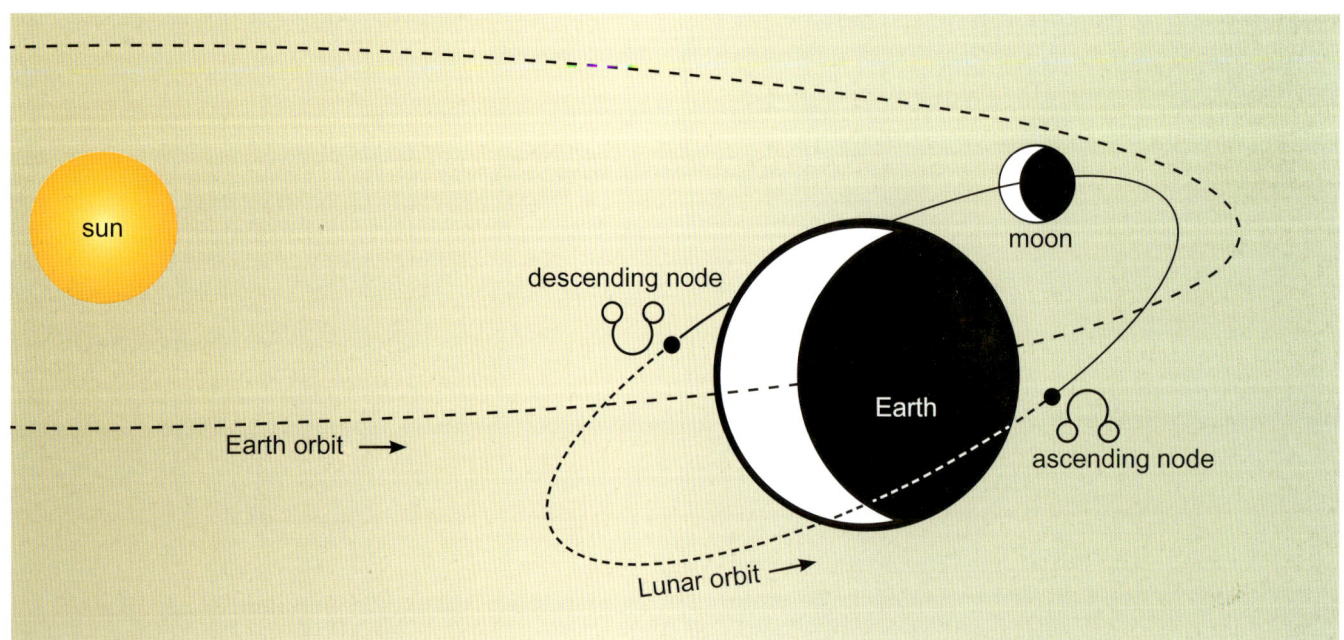

Orbit

It takes the moon the same amount of time to rotate around once as it does for the moon to go around the Earth once. Therefore, Earth-bound observers can never see the 'far-side' of the moon. Tidal forces cause many of the moons of our solar system to have this type of orbit.

The moon's orbit is expanding over time. For example, a billion years ago, the moon was much closer to the Earth (roughly 200,000 km) and took only 20 days to orbit the Earth. Also, one Earth day was about 18 hours long (instead of our 24 hour day). The tides on Earth were also much stronger since the moon was closer to the Earth.

Saros

The saros is the roughly 18-year periodic cycle of the Earth-moon-sun system. Every 6,585 days, the Earth, moon and sun are in exactly the same position. When there is a lunar eclipse, there will also be one exactly 6,585 days later.

Approximately 49 moons can fit into our Earth.

MOON

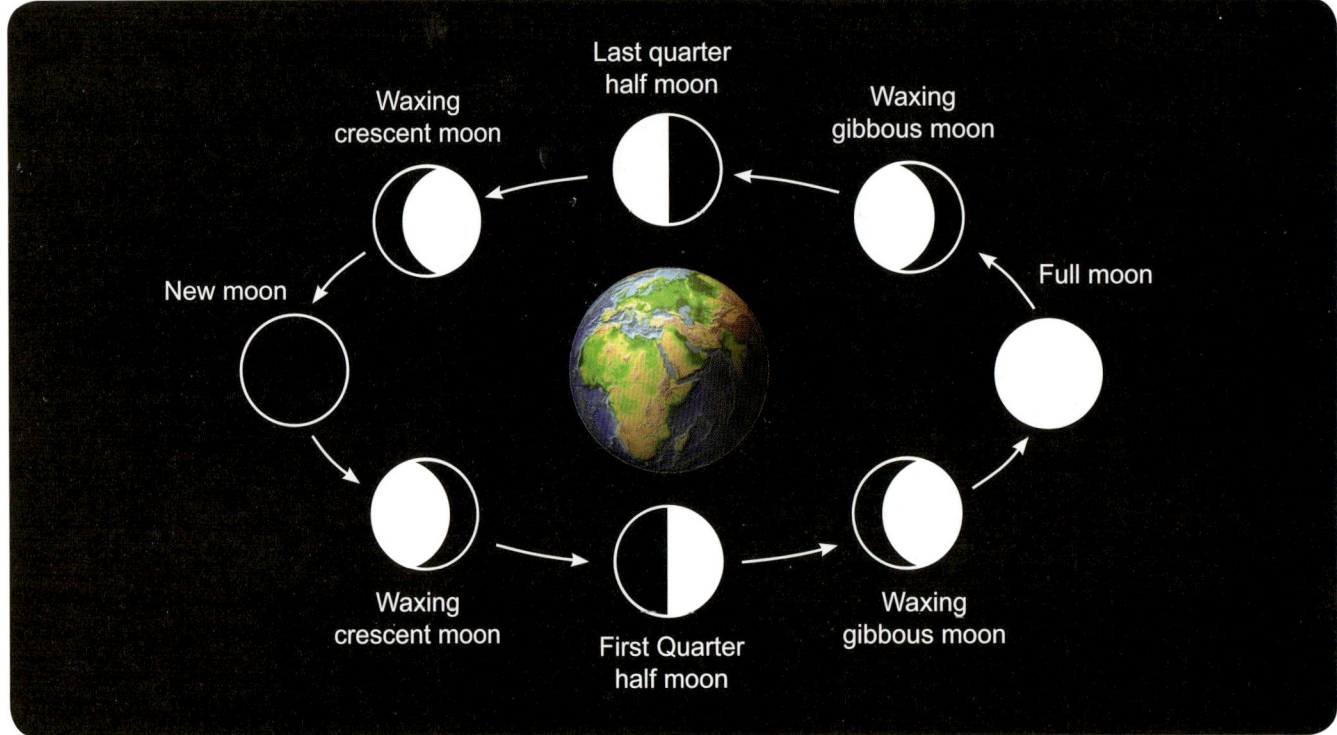

As the moon orbits the Earth, an observer on Earth can see the moon appear to change shape. It seems to change from a crescent to a circle and back again. The shape looks different from one day to the next because the observer sees different parts of the moon's sunlit surface as the moon orbits Earth. The different appearances are known as the **phases of the moon**.

The moon has four phases— new moon, first quarter, full moon and last quarter. When the moon is between the sun and Earth, its sunlit side is turned away from Earth. Astronomers call this darkened phase a new moon.

The next night after a new moon, a thin crescent of light appears along the moon's eastern edge. The remaining portion of the moon that faces Earth is faintly visible because of sunlight reflected from Earth to the moon. Each night, an observer on the Earth can see more of the sunlit side as the line between sunlight and dark, moves westward. After about seven days, the observer can see half a full moon, commonly called a half moon. This phase is known as the **first quarter**. About seven days later, the moon is on the side of Earth opposite the sun. The entire sunlit side of the moon is now visible. This phase is called a **full moon**.

Astonishing fact

The moon is 400 times smaller than the sun, but it is also 400 times closer to Earth. So from Earth, the moon and the sun look about the same size.

About seven days after a full moon, the observer again sees a half moon. This phase is the last quarter or third quarter. After another seven days, the moon is between Earth and the sun, and another new moon occurs.

As the moon changes from new moon to full moon, and more and more of it becomes visible, it is said to be **waxing**. As it changes from full moon to new moon, and less and less of it can be seen, it is **waning**. When the moon appears smaller than a half moon, it is called **crescent**. When it looks larger than a half moon, but is not yet a full moon, it is called **gibbous**.

Like the sun, the moon rises in the east and sets in the west. As the moon progresses through its phases, it rises and sets at different times. In the new moon phase, it rises with the sun and travels close to the sun across the sky.

> The entire surface of the moon is covered in a layer of crushed and powdered rocks called the regolith. The dust is a result of millions of years of bombardment from space by tiny micrometeorites.

MOON

Eclipses occur when Earth, the sun and the moon are in a straight line or nearly so. A **lunar eclipse** occurs when the Earth gets directly or almost directly between the sun and the moon, and Earth's shadow falls on the moon. A lunar eclipse can occur only during a full moon. A solar eclipse occurs when the moon gets directly or almost directly between the sun and Earth, and the moon's shadow falls on Earth. A **solar eclipse** can occur only during a new moon.

During one part of each lunar orbit, the Earth is between the sun and the moon and during another part of the orbit; the moon is between the sun and Earth. But in most cases, the astronomical bodies are not aligned directly enough to cause an eclipse. Instead, Earth casts its shadow into space above or below the moon, or the moon casts its shadow into space above or below Earth.

Astonishing fact

An annular eclipse occurs when the moon is too small to block the whole sun and leaves a ring of light visible. This eclipse happens because the moon's orbit is not a perfect circle, so when the moon is farthest away from Earth, it appears smaller in the sky.

As the moon circles the Earth, the shape of the moon appears to change. This is because different amounts of the illuminated part of the moon are facing us. The shape varies from a full moon (when the Earth is between the sun and the moon) to a new moon (when the moon is between the sun and the Earth).

Blue moon

When two full moons occur in a single month, the second full moon is called a '**Blue** moon.' Another definition of the blue moon is the third full moon that occurs in a season of the year which has four full moons (usually each season has only three full moons).

Crescent moon

A crescent moon is part way between a half moon and a new moon or between a new moon and a half moon.

Full moon

A full moon appears as an entire circle in the sky. The full moon is given different names, depending on when it appears. For example, the 'Harvest moon' is the full moon that appears nearest to the Autumnal Equinox, occurring in late September or early October.

Astonishing fact

A full day on the moon, from one sunrise to the next, lasts about 29 Earth days on average.

Gibbous moon

A gibbous moon is between a full moon and a half moon.

Half moon

A half moon looks like half a circle. It is sometimes called a quarter moon. This moon has completed one quarter of an orbit around the Earth from either the full or new position and one quarter of the moon's surface is visible from the Earth.

New moon

The new moon is the phase of the moon when the moon is not visible from the Earth, because the side of the moon that is facing us is not being lit by the sun.

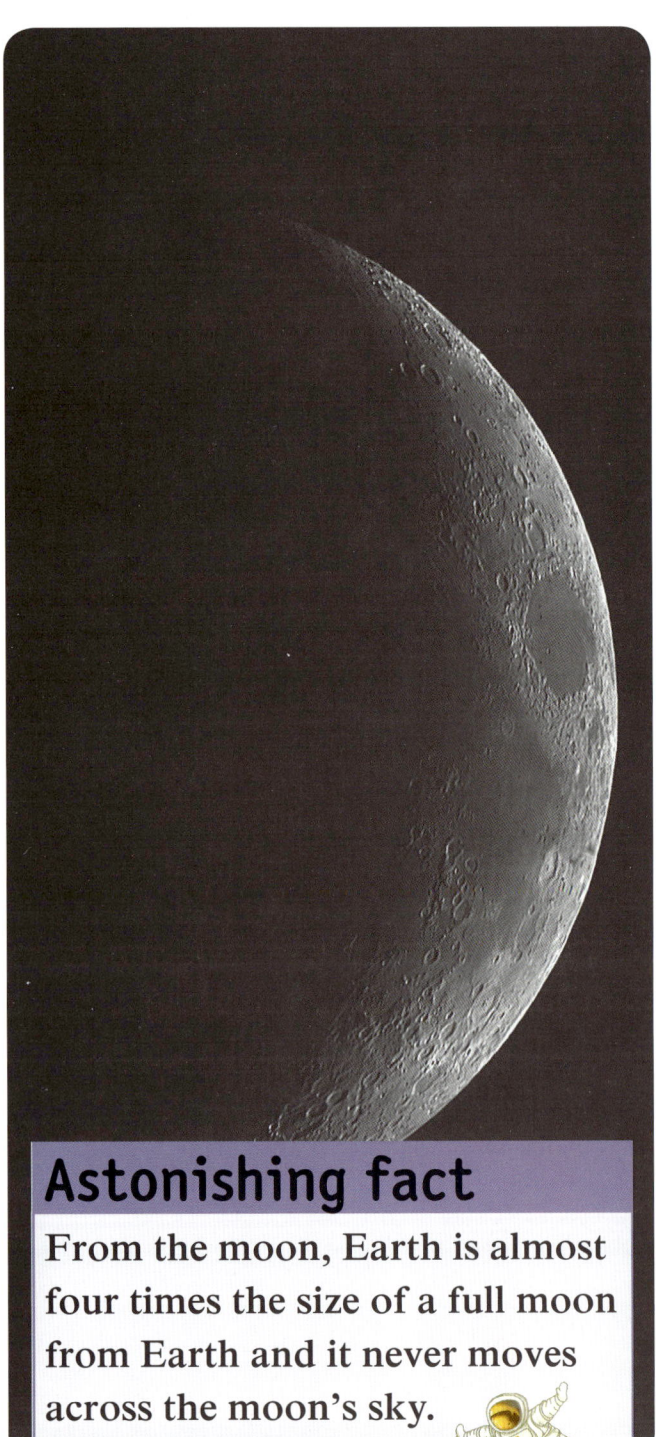

Astonishing fact

From the moon, Earth is almost four times the size of a full moon from Earth and it never moves across the moon's sky.

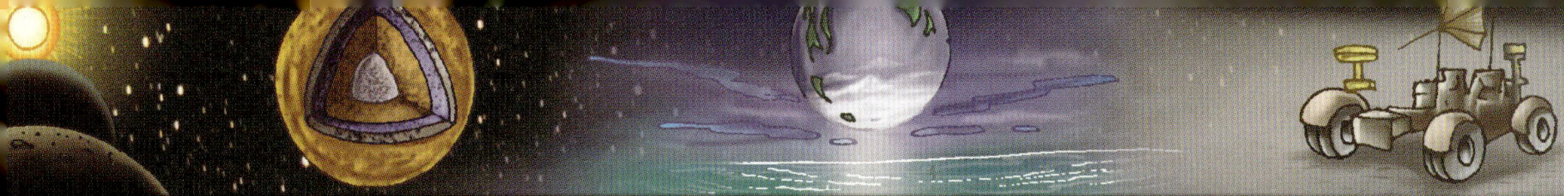

Relation with the Earth

The moon and the Earth are held together by gravity. The Earth is much more massive than the moon causing the moon to orbit the Earth. The moon revolves eastwards (counter clockwise). Each orbit takes 27.3 days. The moon also rotates or spins on an internal axis once every 27.3 days. The rotation and revolution of the moon is the same generally due to gravitational attraction of the moon to the Earth. It makes one rotation per revolution.

The moon's orbit around the Earth is slightly elliptical or oval-shaped. At its closest point called **perigee**, the moon is 363,000 km from the Earth. At its maximum distance called **apogee**, the moon is 405,000 km away. Apogee and perigee are highly elliptical.

Astonishing fact

As there is no atmosphere on the moon, there is no twilight before nightfall.

There are at least three reasons why the orbits of the moon and Earth are elliptical. First, due to their rotation, both bodies are slightly wider at the equator than between the poles. They are not perfect spheres, which makes their orbits a little erratic. Second, it is also possible that moon's internal structure is slightly uneven, which would also contribute to an elliptical orbit.

MOON

The gravitational forces between the Earth and the moon cause some interesting effects. The most obvious is the tides. The moon's gravitational attraction is stronger on the side of the Earth nearest to the moon and weaker on the opposite side. The gravitational pull of the moon tugs on the surface of the ocean until its water surface mounds up and outward in the direction of the moon. When the mound of water has reached its highest point it is called **high tide**. On the opposite side of the Earth from the moon, the centrifugal force caused by the Earth's rotation produces another mound of water and high tide. Between these two high tides are two flat areas on the surface of the ocean which are the low tides.

Each day there are two high tides and two low tides. The time between high and low tide is a little over 6 hours and the entire tidal cycle repeats itself four times each day. The regularity of the tides corresponds to the regular orbit of the moon around the Earth and the rotation of the Earth as it orbits around the sun.

Astonishing fact

The first person to draw a map of the moon as it appears through a telescope was British astronomer Thomas Harriot (c. 1560-1621).

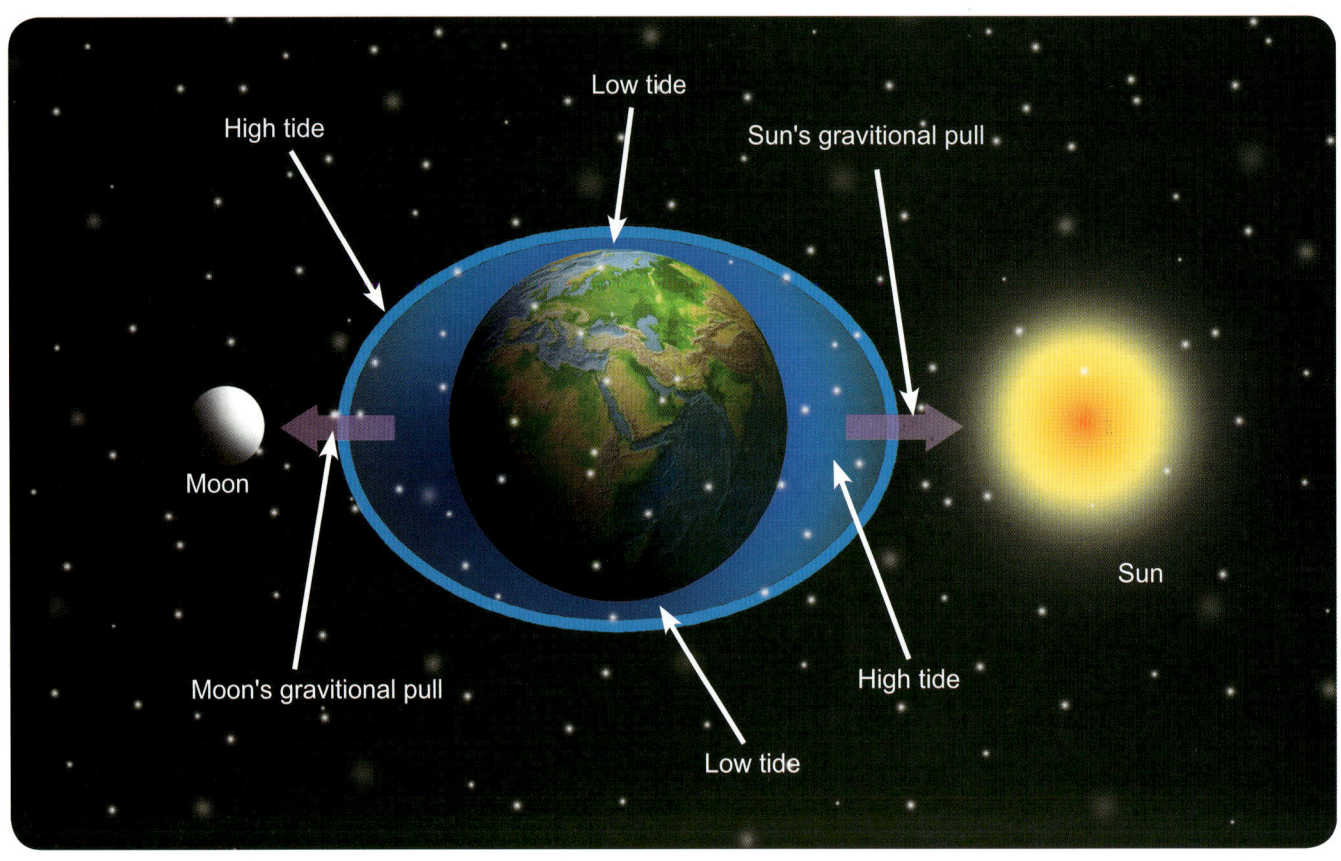

Study and exploration

Some Greek philosophers believed that the moon was a world much like Earth. In about A.D. 100, Plutarch even suggested that people lived on the moon. The Greeks also apparently believed that the dark areas of the moon were seas, while the bright regions were land.

In about A.D. 150, Ptolemy, a Greek astronomer said that the moon was Earth's nearest neighbour in space. He thought that both the moon and the sun orbited Earth. Ptolemy's views survived for more than 1,300 years. But by the early 1500's, the Polish astronomer Nicolaus Copernicus had developed the correct view—Earth and the other planets revolve around the sun and the moon orbits the Earth.

Astonishing fact

The Earth is 81 times heavier than the moon.

Apollo missions

Beginning in 1959, the Soviet Union and the United States sent a series of robot spacecraft to examine the moon in detail. Their ultimate goal was to land people safely on the moon. The United States finally reached that goal in 1969 with the landing of the Apollo 11 lunar module. The United States conducted six more Apollo missions, including five landings. The last of those was Apollo 17, in December 1972.

The Apollo missions revolutionized the understanding of the moon. Much of the knowledge gained about the moon also applies to Earth and the other inner planets like Mercury, Venus, and Mars. After the Apollo missions, the Soviets sent four Luna robot craft to the moon. The last, Luna 24, returned samples of lunar soil to Earth in August 1976.

MOON

Astonishing fact

A 13,000-year-old eagle bone found in France appears to have served as a counting stick to track the phases of the moon!

In January 1959, a small Soviet sphere bristling with antennas, dubbed **Luna 1**, flew by the moon at a distance of some 5,995 km. Though Luna 1 did not impact the moon's surface, as was likely intended, its suite of scientific equipment revealed for the first time that the moon had no magnetic field. The craft also returned evidence of space phenomena, such as the steady flow of ionized plasma now known as solar wind.

First Landing

Later in 1959 **Luna 2** became the first spacecraft to land on the moon's surface when it impacted near the Aristides, Archimedes, and Autolycus craters. A third Luna mission subsequently captured the first, blurry, images of the far side of the moon.

In 1962 NASA placed its first spacecraft on the moon—**Ranger 4**. The Ranger missions were kamikaze missions (suicidal missions); the spacecraft were engineered to streak straight towards the moon and capture as many images as possible before crashing onto its surface. Unfortunately Ranger 4 was unable to return any scientific data before slamming into the far side of the moon.

Two years later, however, **Ranger 7** streaked toward the moon with cameras blazing and captured more than 4,000 photos in the 17 minutes before it smashed onto the surface. Images from all the Ranger missions, particularly **Ranger 9**, showed that the moon's surface was rough. They spotlighted the challenges of finding a smooth landing site on its surface.

Study and exploration

In 1966 the Soviet spacecraft **Luna 9** overcame the moon's topographic hurdles and became the first vehicle to soft-land safely on the surface. The small craft was stocked with scientific and communications equipment and it photographed a ground level lunar panorama. **Luna 10** launched later that year became the first spacecraft to successfully orbit the moon.

The **Surveyor** space probes (1966-68) were the first Nasa craft to perform controlled landings on the moon's surface. Surveyor carried cameras to explore the moon's surface terrain, as well as soil samplers that analyzed the nature of lunar rock and dirt.

In 1966 and 1967 Nasa launched **lunar orbiters** that were designed to circle the moon and chart its surface in preparation for future manned landings. In total, five lunar orbiter missions photographed about 99 per cent of the moon's surface.

Man on the moon

These robotic probes paved the way for a giant leap forward in space exploration. On July 20, 1969, **Neil Armstrong** and **Edwin 'Buzz' Aldrin** became the first people to reach the moon when their **Apollo 11** lunar lander touched down in the Sea of Tranquility.

Astonishing fact

Aristotle and Pliny the Elder, the well-known Roman naturalist and author believed that a full moon affected the water in a human's brain, causing insanity or irrational behaviour.

Later missions carried a lunar rover that was driven across the satellite's surface, and saw astronauts spend as long as three days on the moon! Before the Apollo project ended in 1972, five other missions and a dozen men had visited the moon.

Astonishing fact

On November 17, 1970, the Soviet robot Lunokhod 1 (meaning 'the moon walker' in Russian) was the first vehicle to travel on the moon.

In 1994, Nasa again focused on the moon. The **Clementine** mission succeeded in mapping the moon's surface in wavelengths other than visible light, from ultraviolet to infrared.

Today India, China, and Japan all have lunar exploration projects in development. The United States own plan is perhaps the most ambitious—to return humans to the moon by 2020 and eventually use the moon as a staging point for human flight to Mars and beyond.

Moon in mythology

The moon has figured in human mythologies, often as a counterpart of the sun. In ancient times, it was not uncommon for cultures to believe that the moon died each night, thus descending into the underworld; other cultures believed that the moon chased the sun (and vice-versa).

The moon has figured prominently in various mythologies and folk beliefs. The numerous lunar deities are often female such as the Greek goddesses Selene and Artemis, their Roman equivalents Luna and Diana or the Thracian Bendis. However, males are also found, such as Nanna or Sin of the Mesopotamians, Thoth of the Egyptians and the Japanese god Susanowo and Tecciztecatl of the Aztecs.

The moon has a long association with insanity and irrationality. The words lunacy and loony are derived from the Latin name for the moon, Luna. Folklore also stated that shape shifters such as werewolves and weretigers, mythical creatures capable of changing form between human and beast, drew their power from the moon and would change into their bestial form during the full moon.

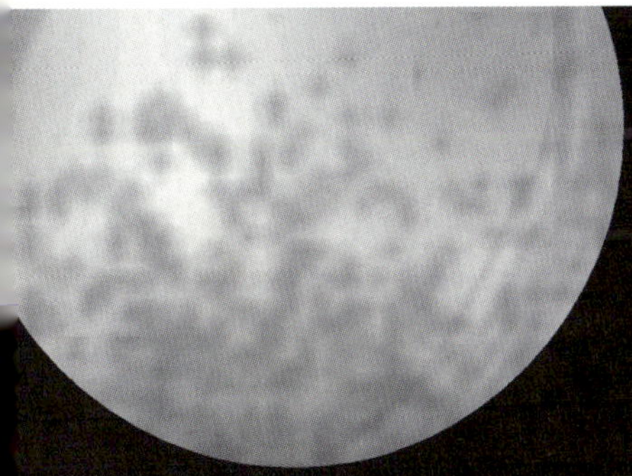

Di you know that the phrase 'once in a blue moon' traditionally refers to an impossible event or an event that rarely happens.

MOON

Many cultures around the world have interesting myths about the moon, reflecting its prominence in the night sky and its impact on our lives.

For thousands of years, humankind has charted life and living by the cycles of the moon. Farmers have planned their planting and harvesting cycles around the moon cycles. Hunters have hunted by the moon's phases, and fishermen in certain cultures have found that their biggest catch happens at the full moon. Priests and priestesses have planned ceremonies to coincide with the full or new moon.

It has also been found that in cultures which honour the cycles of the moon, women are held in a much higher regard than those women in cultures who do not honour the moon phases. Many ancient calendars were actually lunar based; so they had thirteen months, and to this day, several holidays are still dated according to the moon's phase (Easter, Passover and Ramadan).

Many ancient cultures named the full moons according to the time of year.

Astonishing fact

In astrology, the moon represents the inner nature of a person. The moon sign reveals a person's emotional and subconscious state. In Western astrology, the moon is associated to the maternal, while the sun is associated with fatherhood.

Test Your MEMORY

1. What is the moon?

2. Write briefly about how the moon was formed.

3. What is the moon composed of?

4. Write about the craters on the moon.

5. Describe two physical characteristics of the moon.

6. Write about the rotation and orbit of the moon.

7. Describe the phases of the moon.

8. Write in brief about the interior of the moon.

9. How is moon related to the Earth?

10. Write briefly about the history of moon study.

11. Write about some important moon missions.

12. Write about the role of moon in mythology.

Index

A
aluminum 7
apogee 23
asteroids 13, 15
atmosphere 4, 11, 13
axis 14, 16, 23

B
basalt 4, 7, 10
basaltic magmas 9
blue moon 21
breccia 4, 7

C
calcium 7
collision 5, 15
comets 13, 15
core 8, 10, 15
craters 4, 6, 13, 15, 26
crescent moon 18, 21
crust 5, 6, 8

E
eclipses 16, 20
evolution 6

F
full moon 12, 18, 19, 20, 21, 22, 29, 30

G
gibbous moon 18, 22
gravity 12, 23

H
half moon 18, 19, 21, 22
helium 7
highlands 13
hydrogen 7

L
libration 14
lunar eclipse 17, 20
lunar orbiters 27
lunar rover 28

M
magma 5
magnesium 7, 9
magnetic field 10, 15, 26
mantle 5, 8, 9
mare 13, 9
maria 6, 13
meteorites 4, 6, 13
minerals 7, 9
moonquakes 8

P
perigee 23

R
regolith 8
rille 13

S
saros 17
satellite 3, 10
Sea of Tranquility 13, 27
silicon 7
solar eclipse 16, 20
solar system 3, 12, 15, 16, 17
spherical 3

T
tides 12, 17, 24
titanium 7

V
vesicles 10

W
waning 14, 19
waxing 14, 19
weather 4

PEGASUS ENCYCLOPEDIA LIBRARY

Space

STARS

Edited by: Pallabi B. Tomar, Hitesh Iplani
Managing editor: Tapasi De
Designed by: Vijesh Chahal, Anil Kumar, Rohit Kumar
Illustrated by: Suman S. Roy, Tanoy Choudhury
Colouring done by: Vinay Kumar, Kiran Kumari & Pradeep Kumar

CONTENTS

Introduction 3

Evolution of stars 5

What are stars made of? 9

Characteristics of stars 11

Types of stars 13

Twinkling of stars 17

The colour of stars 19

Naming stars 21

Distribution of stars 22

Classification of stars 24

Studying and watching stars 27

Some brightest stars 29

Test Your Memory 31

Index 32

Introduction

For thousands of years, human beings have looked at the night sky and wondered about the things they saw. Ancient people believed they could see shapes among the stars. They identified both animals and people and each had its own story. These chance alignments of the stars are known as **constellations**. Today, 88 constellations are used by astronomers to organize the night sky and to identify the locations of the stars. Stars are the most plentiful objects in the visible universe. They provide the light and energy that fuels a solar system. They also create the heavy elements that are necessary to form life. Without stars, there would be no life. The sun provides energy for nearly every living thing on Earth. It also warms our planet's surface to create a virtual oasis in the coldness of space.

Astonishing fact

Double stars are two stars that look like one to the naked eye but separate in a telescope view.

What is a star?

A star is a huge, shining ball in space that produces a tremendous amount of light and other forms of energy. The sun is a star, and it supplies Earth with light and heat energy. The stars look like twinkling points of light except for the sun. The sun looks like a ball because it is much closer to Earth than any other star.

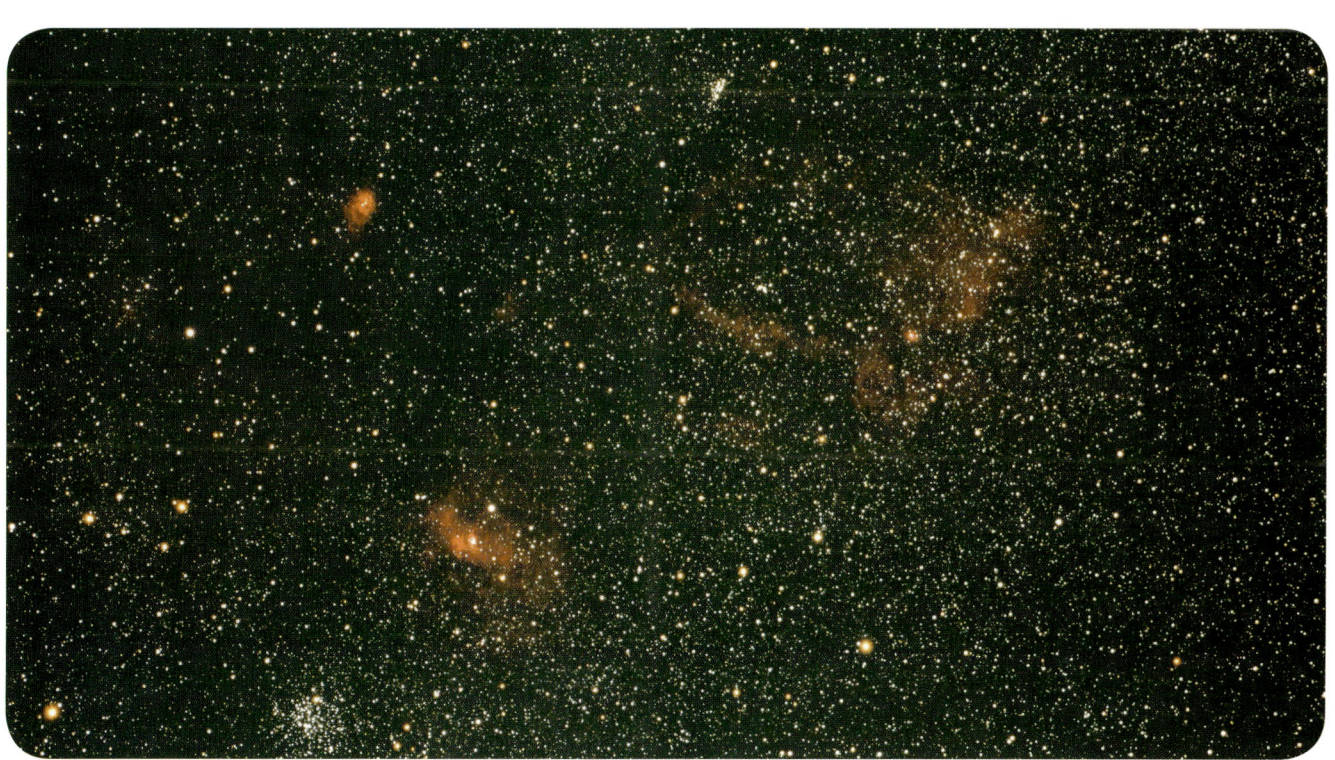

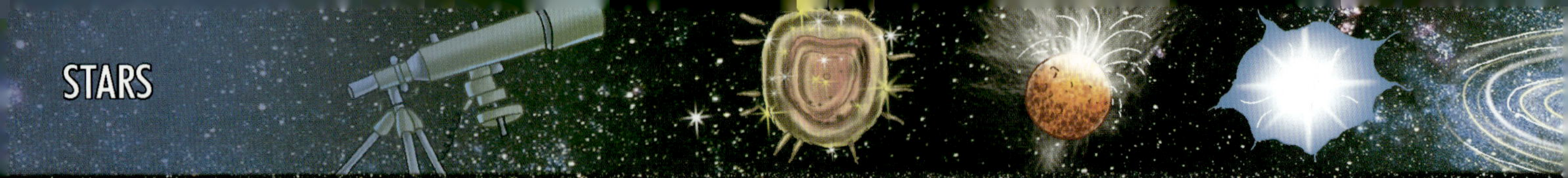

STARS

To many people, a star is simply one of many bright glowing lights in the sky at night. In reality, stars are much more complex. A star is actually a self-luminous celestial body consisting of a mass of gas that is held together by its own gravity. The glowing light typically seen from Earth is caused by actual nuclear reactions occurring within the stars core. These nuclear reactions are balanced by the outflow of energy to the surface of the star which produces the glow we so commonly associate with stars here on Earth.

Stars are cosmic energy engines that produce heat, light, ultraviolet rays, x-rays, and other forms of radiation. They are composed largely of gas and plasma, a superheated state of matter composed of subatomic particles.

No one knows how many stars exist, but the number would be staggering. Our universe likely contains more than 100 billion galaxies and each of those galaxies may have more than 100 billion stars!

Astonishing fact

When an average-sized star dies, it sheds its outer layers, which causes the formation of planetary nebula. The Cat's Eye Nebula is the best example of a planetary nebula.

Evolution of stars

It is common knowledge, that a bright star is also the hottest one and the small or dim ones are the coolest stars. Depending on this primary hypothesis, a star is studied for further information about its origin. Stars like **Vega** are a huge mass of cold and dusty clouds made up of gases. The gravitational force causes the gases to contract. The assembling of matter in close formations leads to a rise in temperature. This rise in temperature leads to a chain of nuclear reactions in the atoms of the components present. The reason why we see luminous bodies in space is because of the energy released during chemical reactions in the stellar area.

The dusty mass consists of a large amount of hydrogen. The nucleus of a hydrogen atom undergoes a nuclear fusion reaction, to transform into helium. This conversion is accompanied by a steady release of a huge amount of energy. This is visible as a radiant light in space. This sequence of events lasts for about 10 billion years in the case of an average or medium sized star. For instance, the sun (which is a medium sized star) is believed to be 5 billion years old and may live on for another 5 billion years!

Astonishing fact

The constellation of Cygnus (Swan) contains the very biggest star in the known universe—a hyper giant which is almost a million times as big as the sun!

STARS

Stars form when cool, relatively dense clouds (molecular clouds) of interstellar gas and dust shrink upon themselves as a result of gravitational collapse. In a spiral galaxy such as the Milky Way, star formation is usually triggered when gas clouds are compressed by shock waves.

The birthplace of stars

Stars are born in regions of unstable clouds of dust and gas which are scattered throughout the outer spiral arms of our Milky Way. Hundreds of newborn stars are nursed in the Orion Nebula, which is just visible to the naked eye as a fuzzy speck of light in the constellation of Orion. However, the lit up regions of the nebula only represent a small portion, as much of the nebula is actually full of dense molecular clouds which absorb visible light and can only be probed with radio waves.

Evolution of stars

The formation of stars

Once the clouds start to collapse, the material breaks down into massive lumps, and as these continue to collapse, gravitational compression causes the lumps of cloud to warm up as gravitational potential energy is converted into heat. It is these lumps that will eventually form a single star, two stars or even a star with its own planetary system.

As the pressure and temperature increases in these lumps, a sphere made up of superhot gas called a **proto-star** (a potential star) is formed. This proto-star will continue to collapse until its core approaches close to 10 million Kelvin's as that is the required temperature to undergo nuclear fusion.

Astonishing fact

True binary stars are two stars held together by one another's gravity, which spend their lives whirling around together like a pair of dancers!

The entire formation process of a star like our sun, might take about 50 million years. Once a star has begun the conversion of hydrogen into helium, the remainder of its life will be determined exclusively by its mass. This nuclear reaction releases heat and produces an outward pressure which supports and holds up the star against further gravitational collapse for as long as there is enough nuclear fuel to burn.

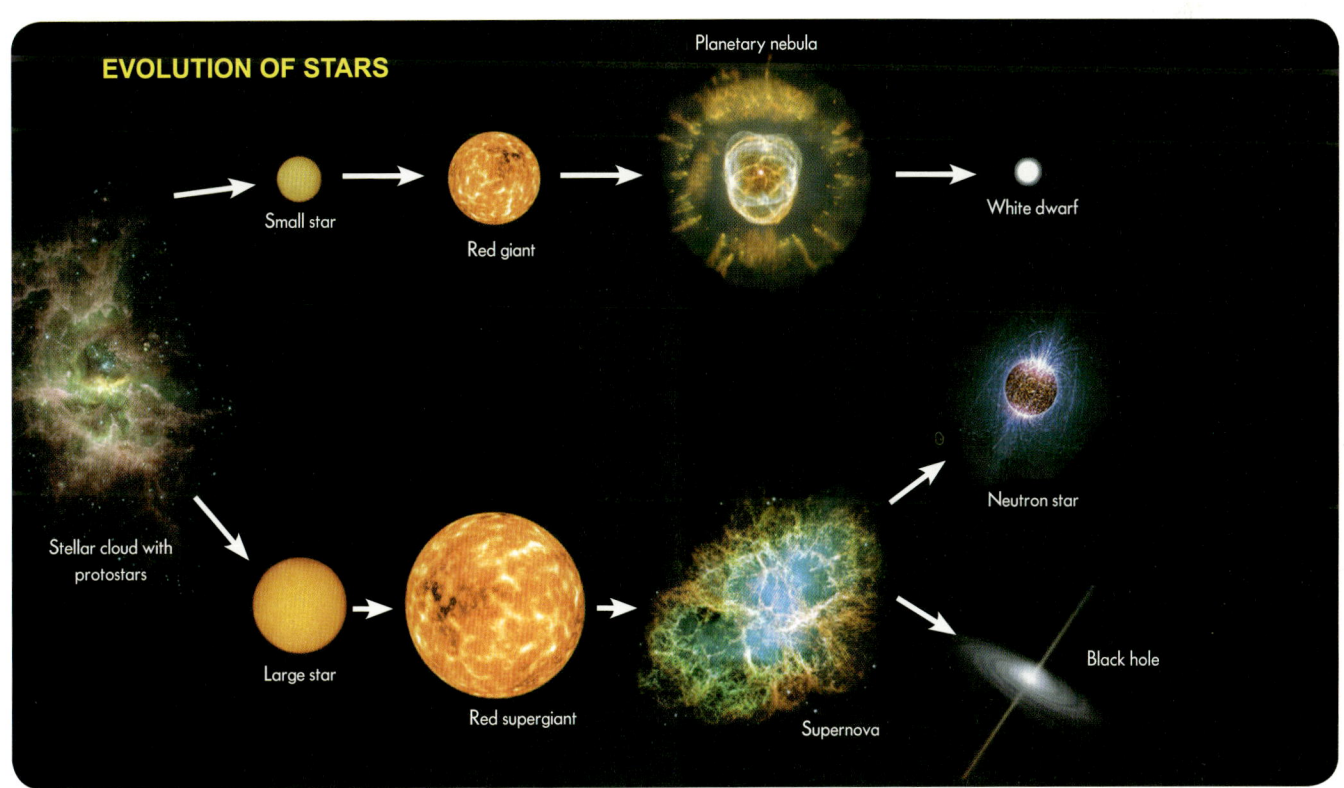

EVOLUTION OF STARS

STARS

The end of an era

After exhausting all readily available hydrogen in its core, nuclear fusion comes to a halt and the core begins to contract due to gravity. Stars with masses between 0.5 and 8 solar masses (1 solar mass is the mass of the sun) expand to become **red giants**.

These massive stars have a radius several hundred times the size of our sun and each will ultimately expel its outer shell. The expelled material is called a **planetary nebula** as it resembles a giant planet when observed through an optical telescope. This ring of expelled material will remain visible for about 10 thousand years before gradually dispersing into interstellar space. The star is now dead as it has no fuel. All that is left is a **white dwarf star**.

A violent death

The evolution of stars with masses greater than 8 solar masses is not as pleasant but much more dramatic. As a result of their sheer size, these stars burn through their hydrogen supply at a faster rate but at the cost of a considerably shortened lifespan. Once their hydrogen to helium conversion phase is over, they expand to become red **supergiants**.

These are the largest stars in existence in terms of radii. Once, all its energy is spent, the red supergiant collapses and explodes as a **supernova**, shining briefly with the light of a billion suns. Most of this material is expelled into space. All that remains is a spherical body of incredible density which will either collapse into a **neutron star** or possibly, a **black hole**.

Astonishing fact

The sun is about 5 billion years old and half way through its life. As a medium sized star it will probably live for another 10 billion years.

What are stars made of?

Stars are made of the same stuff as the rest of the Universe: 73 per cent hydrogen, 25 per cent helium, and the last 2 per cent are all the other elements.

After the Big Bang, 13.7 billion years ago, the entire Universe was a hot dense sphere. The conditions inside this young Universe were so hot that it was equivalent to being inside the core of a star. In other words, the entire Universe was like a star. And for the brief time that the Universe was in this state, nuclear fusion reactions converted hydrogen into helium to the ratios we see today.

The Universe kept expanding and cooling down, and eventually the hydrogen and helium cooled down to the point that it could actually start collecting together with its mutual gravity. This is how the first stars were born. And just like the stars we have today, they were made up of roughly 73 per cent hydrogen and 25 per cent helium. These first stars were enormous and probably detonated as supernova within a million years of forming. In their life, and in their death, these first stars created some of the heavier elements that we have here on Earth, like oxygen, carbon, gold and uranium.

Astonishing fact

The brightest stars in the night sky are not actually stars, but the planets Jupiter, Venus, Mars and Mercury.

STARS

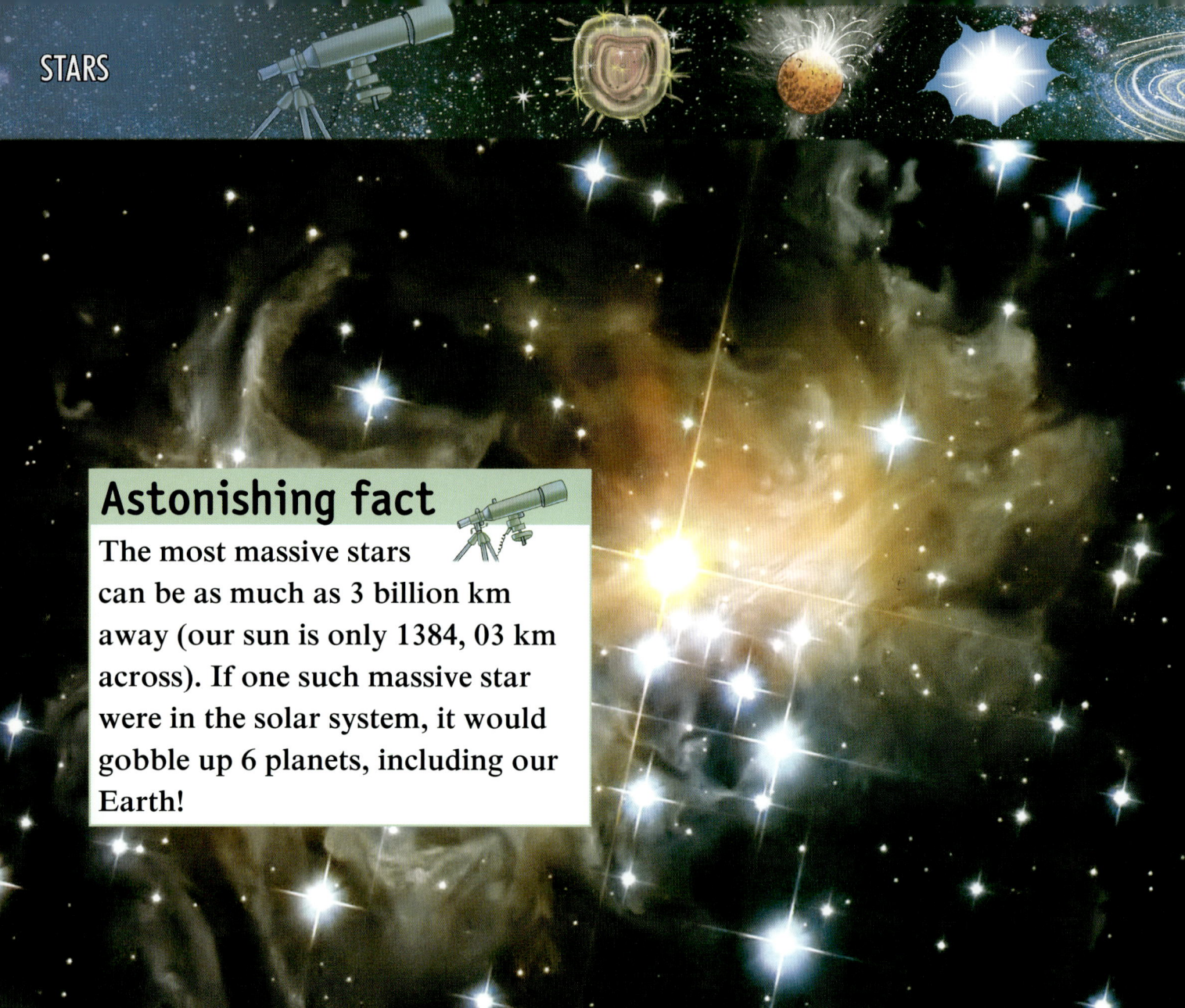

Astonishing fact

The most massive stars can be as much as 3 billion km away (our sun is only 1384, 03 km across). If one such massive star were in the solar system, it would gobble up 6 planets, including our Earth!

Stars have been forming since the Universe began. In fact, astronomers calculate that 5 new stars form in the Milky Way every year. Some have more of the heavier elements left over from previous stars; these are metal-rich stars. Others have less of these elements; the metal-poor stars. But even so, the ratio of elements is still roughly the same. Our own sun is an example of a metal rich star with a higher than average amount of heavier elements inside it. And yet, the sun's ratios are very similar; 71 per cent hydrogen, 27.1 per cent helium, and then the rest as heavier elements, like oxygen, carbon, nitrogen, etc. Of course, the sun has been converting hydrogen into helium in its core for 4.5 billion years.

Stars everywhere are made of the same stuff—3/4 hydrogen and 1/4 helium. It's the stuff left over from the formation of the universe and one of the most elegant pieces of evidence to help explain how we are here today.

Characteristics of stars

A star is a massive ball of plasma that emits light throughout the universe. A star can be defined by five basic characteristics— brightness, colour, surface temperature, size and mass.

Brightness

Two characteristics define brightness— **luminosity** and **magnitude.** Luminosity is the amount of light that a star radiates. The size of the star and its surface temperature determines its luminosity. Apparent magnitude of a star is its visible brightness, factoring in size and distance, while absolute magnitude is its true brightness irrespective of its distance from Earth.

Colour

A star's colour depends on its surface temperature. Cooler stars tend to be redder in colour, while hotter stars have a bluer appearance. Stars in the mid ranges are white or yellow such as our sun. Stars can also blend colours, such as red-orange stars or blue-white stars.

Astonishing fact

Betelgeuse, the bright star on Orion's top-left shoulder, is so big that if it was placed where the sun is, it would swallow up Earth, Mars and Jupiter!

11

STARS

Astonishing fact

It's estimated that the number of stars in the universe is greater than the number of grains of sand on all the beaches in the world!

Surface temperature

Astronomers measure a star's temperature on the Kelvin scale (K). Zero degree on the Kelvin scale is equal to -273.15 degrees Celsius. The coolest, reddest stars are approximately 2,500 K, while the hottest stars can reach upto 50,000 K. Our sun is about 5,500 K.

Size

Astronomers measure the size of a given star in terms of our own sun's radius. Thus, a star that measure 1 solar radii would be the same size as our sun. The star Rigel, which is much larger than our sun, measures 78 solar radii. A star's size, along with its surface temperature determines its luminosity.

Mass

A star's mass is also measured in terms of our own sun, with 1 equal to the size of our sun. For instance, Rigel, which is much larger than our sun, has a mass of 3.5 solar masses. Two stars of a similar size may not necessarily have the same mass, as stars can vary greatly in density.

Types of stars

Main Sequence Stars

The main sequence is the point in a star's evolution during which it maintains a stable nuclear reaction. It is this stage during which a star will spend most of its life. Our sun is a main sequence star. A **main sequence star** will experience only small fluctuations in luminosity and temperature. The amount of time a star spends in this phase depends on its mass. Large, massive stars will have a short main sequence stage while less massive stars will remain in main sequence much longer. Very massive stars will exhaust their fuel in only a few hundred million years. Smaller stars, like the sun, will burn for several billion years during their main sequence stage. Very massive stars will become blue giants during their main sequence.

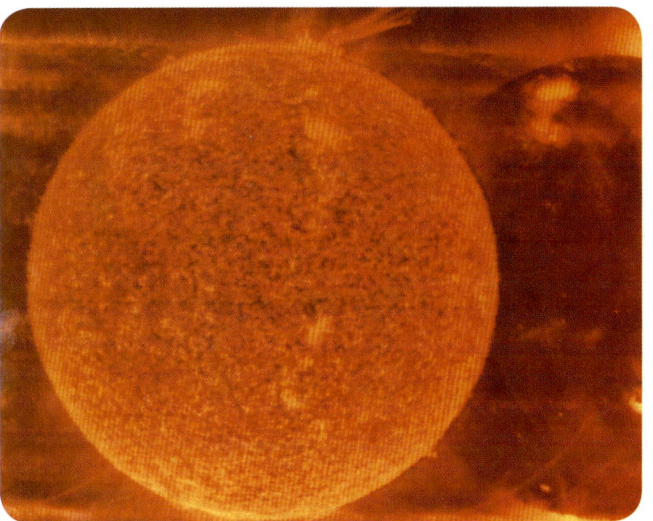
Red Giant Stars

Red Giant Stars

A **red giant** is a large star that is reddish or orange in colour. It represents the late phase of development in a star's life, when its supply of hydrogen has been exhausted and helium is being fused. This causes the star to collapse, raising the temperature in the core. The outer surface of the star expands and cools, giving it a reddish colour. Red giants are very large, reaching sizes of over 100 times the star's original size.

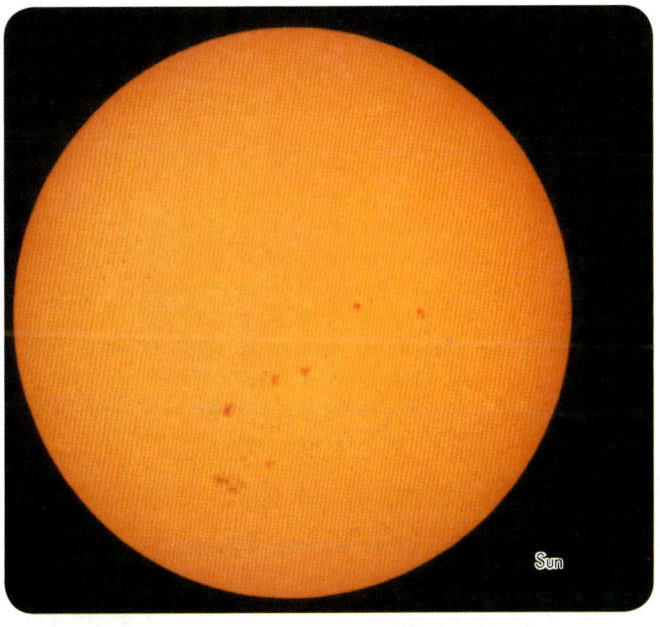

Astonishing fact

Our galaxy has approximately 250 billion stars and it is estimated by astronomers that there are 100 billion other galaxies in the universe!

13

White Dwarf Stars

A **white dwarf** is the remnant of an average-sized star that has passed through the red giant stage of its life after the star has used up its remaining fuel. At this point the star may expel some of its matter into space, creating a planetary nebula. What remains is the dead core of the star. Nuclear fusion no longer takes place. The core glows because of its residual heat. Eventually the core will radiate all of its heat into space and cool down to become what is known as a black dwarf. White dwarf stars are very dense. Their size is about the same as that of the Earth, but they contain as much mass as the sun. They are extremely hot, reaching temperatures of over 100,000 degrees!

Blue Giant Stars

Blue giants blaze with a surface temperature of 20,000 K or more and are extremely luminous. Just for comparison, a star like our sun only has a surface temperature of about 6,000 K. A blue giant star can emit 10,000 times as much energy as the sun.

As the blue stars are large and compact, they burn their fuel quickly, which gives them a very high temperature. These stars often run out of fuel in only 10,000-100,000 years.

White dwarf stars

> All of the stars comprising the Milky Way galaxy revolve around the centre of the galaxy once every 200 million years or so.

Types of stars

Variable Stars

A **variable star** is a star that changes in brightness. These fluctuations can range from seconds to years depending on the type of variable star. Stars usually change their brightness when they are young and when they are old and dying. They are classified as either intrinsic or extrinsic. Intrinsic variables change their brightness because of conditions within the stars themselves. Extrinsic variables change brightness because of some external factor, like an orbiting companion star. These are also known as eclipsing binaries.

Binary Stars

Many stars in the universe are part of a multiple star system. A **binary star** is a system of two stars that are gravitationally bound to each other. They orbit around a common point, called the centre of mass. It is estimated that about half of all the stars in our galaxy are part of a binary system.

Binary stars

Variable stars

Astonishing fact

The oldest star yet discovered is HE which is 13.2 billion years old!

Stars

Red Dwarf Stars

Red dwarf stars are the most common kind of stars in the Universe. These are main sequence stars but they have such low mass that they're much cooler than stars like our sun. They have another advantage. Red dwarf stars are able to keep the hydrogen fuel mixing into their core, and so they can conserve their fuel for much longer than other stars. Astronomers estimate that some red dwarf stars will burn for up to 10 trillion years. The smallest red dwarfs are 0.075 times the mass of the sun, and they can have a mass of up to half of the sun.

Neutron stars

Neutron Stars

If a star has between 1.35 and 2.1 times the mass of the sun, it doesn't form a white dwarf when it dies. Instead, the star dies in a catastrophic supernova explosion, and the remaining core becomes a neutron star. As its name implies, a neutron star is an exotic type of star that is composed entirely of neutrons. This is because the intense gravity of the neutron star crushes protons and electrons together to form neutrons. If stars are even more massive, they will become black holes instead of neutron stars after the supernova goes off.

Supergiant stars

Supergiant Stars

The largest stars in the Universe are **supergiant stars**. These are monsters with dozens of times the mass of the sun. Unlike a relatively stable star like the sun, supergiants consume hydrogen fuel at an enormous rate and will consume all the fuel in their cores within just a few million years. Supergiant stars live fast and die young, detonating as supernova; completely disintegrating themselves in the process.

Astonishing fact
Some stars are 600,000 times as bright as our sun!

Twinkling of stars

Twinkling of stars

If you look at the stars on a clear night, you will notice that they seem to twinkle and that they differ greatly in brightness. A much slower movement also takes place in the night sky. If you map the location of several stars for a few hours, you will observe that all the stars revolve slowly about a single point in the sky.

Twinkling of stars is caused by movements in Earth's atmosphere. Starlight enters the atmosphere as straight rays. Twinkling occurs because air movements constantly change the path of the light as it comes through the air.

How bright a star looks when viewed from Earth depends on two factors—the actual brightness of the star and the distance of the star from the Earth.

A nearby star that is actually dim can appear brighter than a distant star that is really extremely brilliant. For example, Alpha Centauri A seems to be slightly brighter than a star known as Rigel. But Alpha Centauri A emits only 1/100,000 as much light energy as Rigel. Alpha Centauri A seems brighter because it is only 1/325 as far from Earth as Rigel is - 4.4 light-years for Alpha Centauri A, 1,400 light-years for Rigel.

STARS

Polaris or the North Star is the only star in the sky that doesn't appear to move from night to night.

The scientific name for the twinkling of stars is stellar scintillation (or astronomical scintillation). Stars twinkle when we see them from the Earth's surface because we are viewing them through thick layers of turbulent (moving) air in the Earth's atmosphere.

Stars (except for the sun) appear as tiny dots in the sky. As their light travels through the many layers of the Earth's atmosphere, the light of the star is bent (refracted) many times and in random directions (light is bent when it hits a change in density like a pocket of cold air or hot air). This random refraction results in the star winking out (it looks as though the star moves a bit, and our eye interprets this as twinkling).

Stars closer to the horizon appear to twinkle more than stars that are overhead. This is because the light of stars near the horizon has to travel through more air than the light of stars overhead and so is subject to more refraction. Also, planets do not usually twinkle, because they are so close to us; they appear big enough that the twinkling is not noticeable.

18

The colour of stars

The colour of a star depends on its surface temperature. Our sun's surface temperature is about 6,000 K. Although it looks yellow from here on Earth, the light of the sun would actually look very white from space. This white light coming off the sun is because its temperature is 6,000 K. If the sun were cooler, it would give off light more on the red end of the spectrum and if the sun were hotter, it would look bluer.

And that's just what we see with other stars. The coolest stars in the universe are the red dwarf stars. These are stars with just a fraction of the mass of our sun (as low as 7.5% the mass of the sun). They don't burn as hot in their cores, and their surface temperature is about 3,500 K. The light released from their surface looks mostly red to our eyes (although there are different colours mixed up in there too though red is the majority).

Astonishing fact

Shooting stars are stars that collide with Earth as it moves around the sun. They heat up, glow and then burn down. It's common to see one every 15 minutes but they often move so quickly through the air that if you blink, you'll miss them!

STARS

The different colours of the stars are white, red, yellow and blue. The colour of a star determines the temperature of the surface of the star. You need to know that a star emits light in various colours of wavelengths of the electromagnetic spectrum. The surface temperature of a star determines the wavelength of the star. If the surface temperature is around 3,000 K degrees, then the colour of the star is red and if it is orange then the surface temperature is 4,000 K degrees. The colour of a star is yellow when the surface temperature is 6,000 K degrees. When the surface temperature is above 8,000 K degrees, the colour emitted appears white and if the temperature ranges between 20,000 K to 50,000 K degrees, then it is blue.

The wavelengths of blue coloured stars are short and it is an indication that these stars have higher surface temperature. The colours such as red, orange and yellow have longer wavelengths of light indicating that the star's surface temperature is low. The astronomers can determine the surface temperature of the stars by looking at the colours.

Astonishing fact

Of the billions and billions of stars in the universe, only about 6,000 can be seen from the Earth without a telescope.

Naming stars

Ancient people saw that certain stars are arranged in patterns shaped somewhat like human beings, animals or common objects. Some of these patterns called constellations came to represent figures of mythological characters. For example, the constellation Orion (the Hunter) is named after a hero in Greek mythology.

Today, astronomers use constellations, some of which were described by the ancients, in the scientific names of stars. The International Astronomical Union (IAU), the world authority for assigning names to celestial objects, officially recognizes 88 constellations. These constellations cover the entire sky. In most cases, the brightest star in a given constellation has alpha (the first letter of the Greek alphabet) as part of its scientific name.

The second brightest star in a constellation is usually designated beta, the second letter of the Greek alphabet; the third brightest is gamma and so on. The assignment of Greek letters to stars continues until all the Greek letters are used.

But the number of known stars has become so large that the IAU uses a different systems for newly discovered stars. Most new names consist of an abbreviation followed by a group of symbols. The abbreviation stands for either the type of star or a catalog that lists information about the star. For example, PSR J1302-6350 is a type of star known as a pulsar; hence the PSR in its name. The symbols indicate the star's location in the sky. The 1302 and the 6350 are coordinates that are similar to the longitude and latitude designations used to indicate locations on Earth's surface. The J indicates that a coordinate system known as J2000 is being used.

The human eye can detect only a very narrow range of light wavelengths, but stars emit non-visible light as well. And this light can help astronomers determine if 'starlight' actually comes from a star or another celestial body.

21

Distribution of stars

Stars are often found in huge groups called **clusters**. There are two types of clusters, open and globular.

Open clusters have mostly young, bright, blue stars that were born together. They usually have irregular shapes. The most famous open cluster is the **Pleiades**.

At 400 light years away, the Pleiades are the Earth's closest open cluster. You can see the Pleiades without a telescope.

Globular clusters can have as many as a million stars more than open clusters. They tend to have a sphere-like shape, with many stars at the centre. There are 160 globular clusters within the Milky Way. A globular cluster named M15 is the closest of its kind to Earth.

Globular clusters orbit the centre of the Milky Way in a region known as the **galactic halo.** Stars in globular clusters in the galactic halo are the oldest structures in our galaxy. Studying them has helped scientists figure out the age of the galaxy.

A massive star has a shorter lifetime than a less massive star.

Distribution of stars

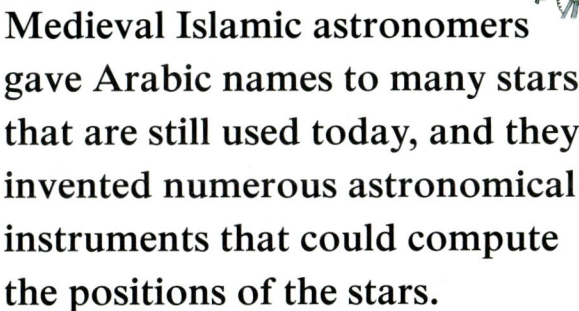

Medieval Islamic astronomers gave Arabic names to many stars that are still used today, and they invented numerous astronomical instruments that could compute the positions of the stars.

Certain stars appear to move in shapes and patterns across the night sky. These patterns are constellations. Some look like animals, humans or objects. Constellations seem to travel in the sky from east to west every night, but they are really not moving. The Earth is moving, rotating on its axis. Constellations also seem to change with the seasons. Again, they are really not changing. They just look that way because Earth is revolving around the sun.

Stars are not spread uniformly across the universe, but are normally grouped into galaxies along with interstellar gas and dust. A typical galaxy contains hundreds of billions of stars, and there are more than 100 billion (10^{11}) galaxies in the observable universe. While it is often believed that stars only exist within galaxies, intergalactic stars have been discovered. Astronomers estimate that there are at least 70 sextillion (7 × 10^{22}) stars in the observable universe! A 2010 estimate revises the star count upward to 300 sextillion (3 × 10^{23})!

Astonishing fact

Some of the stars in the sky are so far that the light from them takes million of years to reach us.

Stars

Classification of stars

Stars have many sizes, ages and temperatures. Most stars do not stay in the same class for their entire life. As a star evolves, it's fuel changes and as a result, its average surface temperature and its size changes. Most stars are mainly sequence stars. These are the medium mass stars. They progress through similar stages as they evolve.

Spectral classification

The most widely used system of classification is spectral classification. Stars radiate light at different frequencies. As nuclear fusion occurs within a star, first hydrogen is used as fuel. The hydrogen is fused into helium, and eventually the star will begin to use helium as fuel. The helium becomes lithium, and so on, and each new, heavier fuel is used in succession. Each element radiates light in different areas of the spectrum. Since each element radiates a unique set of frequencies, this is like a signature that astrophysicists can use to understand what makes up a particular star.

> William Herschel was the first astronomer to attempt to determine the distribution of stars in the sky.

Classification of stars

Astronomers classify stars by colour using a series of letters: O, B, A, F, G, K and M. Under this classification, O stars are the hottest and M stars are the coolest, with the other letters coming in between. O stars are 'blue', A stars are 'white', G stars are 'yellow' and M stars are 'red'.

Since that doesn't provide enough detail, astronomers put a second number after the letter to distinguish where on G, for example, a star like our sun should be positioned. Each number is a further 10 per cent towards the next spectral letter. For example, our sun is classified as a G2 star. This means it's 20 per cent along the way towards an orange main sequence star.

Astronomers use another roman numeral at the end of the spectral letter to define the size and luminosity of a star. They range from I supergiants to V dwarfs, or main sequence stars. As our sun is a main sequence star, it would get the V designation.

So the full classification for the Sun is G2V.

Astonishing fact

Aldebaran is the brightest star in the constellation Taurus and is the 13th brightest star in the sky. It is about 40 times as big as the sun.

STARS

Hertzsprung-Russell diagram

The Hertzsprung-Russell (H-R) diagram is a graph that plots stars colour versus its luminosity. On it, astronomers plot stars' colour, temperature, luminosity, spectral type, and evolutionary stage. This represents a major step towards an understanding of stellar evolution or 'the lives of stars'.

- Most stars, including the sun, are 'main sequence stars,' fuelled by nuclear fusion converting hydrogen into helium. For these stars, the hotter they are, the brighter. These stars are in the most stable part of their existence. This stage generally lasts for about 5 billion years.

- As stars begin to die, they become giants and supergiants. These stars have depleted their hydrogen supply and are very old. The core contracts as the outer layers expand. These stars will eventually explode (becoming a planetary nebula or supernova, depending on their mass) and then become white dwarfs, neutron stars, or black holes, again depending on their mass.

- Smaller stars (like our sun) eventually become faint white dwarfs (hot, white, dim stars) that are below the main sequence. These hot, shrinking stars deplete their nuclear fuels and eventually become cold, dark, black dwarfs.

Astonishing fact

Deneb (which means 'tail' in Arabic) is the brightest star in the constellation Cygnus (the swan). Deneb is about 60,000 times more luminous than the sun!

Studying and watching stars

Historically, stars have been important to civilizations throughout the world. They have been part of religious practices and used for celestial navigation and orientation. Many ancient astronomers believed that stars were permanently affixed to a heavenly sphere, and that they were immutable. By convention, astronomers grouped stars into constellations and used them to track the motions of the planets and the inferred position of the sun. The motion of the sun against the background stars (and the horizon) was used to create calendars, which could be used to regulate agricultural practices. The Gregorian calendar, currently used nearly everywhere in the world, is a solar calendar based on the angle of the Earth's rotational axis relative to its local star, the sun.

The concept of the constellation was known to exist during the Babylonian period. Ancient sky watchers imagined that prominent arrangements of stars formed patterns, and they associated these with particular aspects of nature or their myths. Twelve of these formations lay along the band of the ecliptic and these became the basis of astrology. Many of the more prominent individual stars were also given names, particularly with Arabic or Latin designations.

Astonishing fact

Stars have their own gravity fields, which keep them close to each other. The best example is the globular cluster, which contains millions of stars tightly held by gravity.

STARS

As well as certain constellations and the sun itself, stars as a whole have their own myths. To the Ancient Greeks, some stars represented various important deities, from which the names of the planets Mercury, Venus, Mars, Jupiter and Saturn were taken. (Uranus and Neptune were also Greek and Roman gods, but neither planet was known because of their low brightness. Their names were assigned by later astronomers).

Stars can be observed using many different tools. There are hundreds of different telescopes. There are even probes that help with the job. Probes are large mechanical devices that are used to find things in space. Some radios are tuned all day to pick up a star's movement using radio waves. Even huge telescopes cannot view all stars because some are too far away. Only strong radio waves can detect these stars.

Stellar astronomy is about the study of birth, evolution and finally death of stars. It is an immensely huge subject and occupies a large portion of the main branch of astronomy.

Some brightest stars

Sirius

Sirius

Sirius, also known as the **Dog Star**, is the brightest star in the sky. Its name comes from the Greek word for 'scorching'. It is in the constellation Canis Major (The Great Dog). Sirius is a main sequence star that is about 70 times more luminous than the sun. It is about 8.6 light-years from Earth.

Canopus

Named either for an ancient city in northern Egypt or the helmsman for Menelaus, Canopus is the second brightest star in the sky. It is the brightest star in the southern constellation of Carina and Argo Navis.

Procyon is the eighth brightest star night sky. It is a yellow-white star and at 11.4 light years, one of the closer stars to Earth.

Rigil Kentaurus

Rigel Kentaurus, also known as Alpha Centauri, is the third brightest star in the sky. Its name literally means foot of the centaur. It is actually a triple star system made up of Alpha Centauri A, Alpha Centauri B, and Alpha Centauri C (also known as Proxima Centauri because it is the closet star to Earth at 4.3 light years). Rigel Kentaurus is located in the constellation Centaurus.

Rigil kentaurus

Arcturus

Arcturus is the brightest star in the constellation Bootes, which is one of the oldest constellations in the night sky. It is the fourth brightest star in the entire sky. Arcturus means bear guard, as it overlooks the constellation Ursa Major. It is an orange giant with a diameter about 10 times that of the sun and a luminosity about 100 times that of the sun. At about 34 light-years, Arcturus is one of the nearest giant stars. Arcturus is located in the constellation Bootes.

Vega

Vega is the fifth brightest star in the sky. Its name comes from Arabic meaning 'swooping eagle'. Vega is about 25 light-years from Earth. It is three times the size of the sun and 50 times as luminous. Vega is located in the constellation Lyra.

Capella

The sixth brightest star in the sky, Capella's name comes from Latin meaning little she-goat. Capella is a yellow giant star, like our own sun, but much larger. It is part of a binary star system with a red giant star. The two orbit around each other once every 104 days. Capella is approximately 41 light-years from Earth. Capella is in the constellation Auriga.

Mira (Omicron Ceti) is a well-known variable red giant star in the constellation called Cetus. It was discovered in 1596 by David Fabricus, an amateur Dutch astronomer.

Test Your MEMORY

1. What are stars?

2. Write briefly about the evolution of stars.

3. What are stars made of?

4. Write about two characteristics of stars.

5. Write about the various types of stars.

6. Why do stars twinkle?

7. How does a star look bright?

8. Write about the colour of stars.

9. How are stars named?

10. How are stars distributed in the Universe?

11. How are stars classified?

12. How can stars be studied?

Index

A
alpha 21
Alpha Centauri A 17, 29
Arcturus 30
astronomers 3, 10, 12, 13, 16, 20, 21, 23, 25, 26, 27, 28
Auriga 30

B
beta 21
binary star 7, 15, 30
Bootes 30

C
Canis Major 29
Canopus 29
Capella 30
Carina and Argo Navis 29
clusters 22
constellations 3, 5, 6, 21, 23, 25, 26, 27, 28, 30

G
galaxies 4, 13, 23
gamma 21
gas 4, 6, 7, 23

H
helium 5, 7, 8, 9, 10, 13, 24, 26
Hertzsprung-Russell (H-R) diagram 26
hydrogen 5, 7, 8, 9, 10, 13, 16, 24, 26

I
International Astronomical Union (IAU) 21

K
kelvin scale 12

L
luminosity 11, 12, 13, 25, 26, 30
Lyra 30

M
magnitude 11
main sequence star 13, 24, 25, 26, 29
Milky Way 6, 10, 14, 22

N
neutron star 8, 16
nucleus 5

O
Orion 6, 21
Orion Nebula 6

P
plasma 4, 11
proto-star 7
Proxima Centauri 29

R
radiation 4
red dwarf stars 16, 19
red giants 13, 18
Rigel 12, 17, 29
Rigel Kentaurus 29

S
Sirius 29
solar system 3, 10
stellar classification 24
stellar scintillation 18
supergiant stars 16

T
telescope 3, 8, 20, 22, 28

U
ultraviolet rays 4
Ursa Major 30

V
variable star 15
Vega 5, 30

W
white dwarf stars 14

X
x-rays 4

PEGASUS ENCYCLOPEDIA LIBRARY

Space
SUN

Edited by: Pallabi B. Tomar, Hitesh Iplani
Managing editor: Tapasi De
Designed by: Vijesh Chahal, Anil Kumar, Rohit Kumar
Illustrated by: Suman S. Roy, Tanoy Choudhury
Colouring done by: Vinay Kumar, Kiran Kumari & Pradeep Kumar

CONTENTS

Introduction 3

Formation of the sun 5

Layers of the sun 7

The sun's magnetic field 9

Characteristics of the sun 10

Features 14

Solar eclipse 18

Sunlight 19

Sunrise and sunset 21

Sun's orbit 22

Solar space missions 23

Sun in culture 26

The fate of the sun 29

What the sun does for us 30

Test Your Memory 31

Index 32

Introduction

Astonishing fact
All the coal, oil, gas and wood on Earth would only keep the sun burning only for a few days.

Introduction

Situated at the centre of the solar system, the sun is actually just a large star whose strong magnetic fields cause other solar matter, mainly planets, asteroids, comets, meteoroids and other debris, to orbit around it. The sun is believed to be more than 4.6 billion years old and is comprised of mostly hydrogen (74 per cent) and helium (25 per cent). The remaining 1 per cent is made up of small amounts of various heavier elements.

Life on Earth as we know it, would not be possible without the sun. The solar energy from the sun has supported and sustained terrestrial existence on Earth since the beginning of time. Plants utilize the sun to aid in photosynthesis. Humans and other mammals require energy from the sun for visual light, heat, as well as for powering modern solar devices. The sun is also directly responsible for determining and regulating the varying climates and weather cycles that occur on Earth.

SUN

The sun is the closest star to Earth and is the centre of our solar system. A giant, spinning ball of very hot gas, the sun is fuelled by nuclear fusion reactions. The sun is also an active star that displays sunspots, solar flares, erupting prominences, and coronal mass ejections. In about five billion years, the sun will evolve into a Red Giant and eventually, a White Dwarf star. Many cultures have had interesting myths about the sun, in recognition of its importance to life on Earth.

Only about 5 per cent of stars in the Milky Way are larger than the sun; the vast majority are smaller red dwarf stars. Some of the biggest stars can be 100,000 times brighter and contain 100 times more mass. The sun is also relatively young, a member of the Population I group of stars. Older stars, which formed billions of years before the sun are Population II stars and have less heavier elements in them. The oldest stars are Population III stars, formed just after the Big Bang, but these are purely theoretical.

Astonishing fact

The sun travels around the galaxy once every 200 million years – a journey of 100,000 light years.

Formation of the sun

Though exact information of the formation of the sun is not available, it is believed that it formed between ten and twenty thousand million years ago. As per the astronomers, the hydrogen gas present in the sun came into existence with the 'Big Bang'. In other words, the sun came into being around the same time as the rest of the universe. At the time of the Big Bang, hydrogen gas condensed to form colossal clouds, which later concentrated and formed the numerous galaxies. Some of the hydrogen gas was left free and started floating around in our galaxy.

With time, due to some incident, this free-floating hydrogen gas concentrated and paved way for the formation of the sun and the solar system. Gradually, the sun and the solar system turned into a slowly spinning molecular cloud, composed of hydrogen and helium molecules, along with dust. The cloud started to undergo the process of compression, as a result of its own gravity. Along with the compression, the rotating speed of the cloud became much faster. Its excessive and high-speed spinning ultimately resulted in its flattening into a giant disc.

Astonishing fact

The sun provides our planet with 126,000,000,000,000 horsepower of energy every day!

SUN

Majority of the mass of the disc started collecting right at its centre, resulting in the creation of a gas sphere. The sphere continued to attract material from the disc, which resulted in its further compression. This led to an increase in the temperatures and pressures inside the sphere, which rose to the extent where atoms started fusing in its very centre. This is the point of time when a star—the sun, formed, from the sphere. The rest of the disc, apart from the sphere, turned into planets and the other components of the solar system.

Astonishing fact
More than 1 million Earths would fit inside the sun!

Astronomers think that the hydrogen gas that is now in the sun was created in the Big Bang, when the whole universe came into being. This hydrogen gas formed really giant clouds at that time, and those clouds concentrated and formed galaxies. Some of the hydrogen gas floated around in our own galaxy until something made it concentrate and form the sun and the solar system.

Layers of the sun

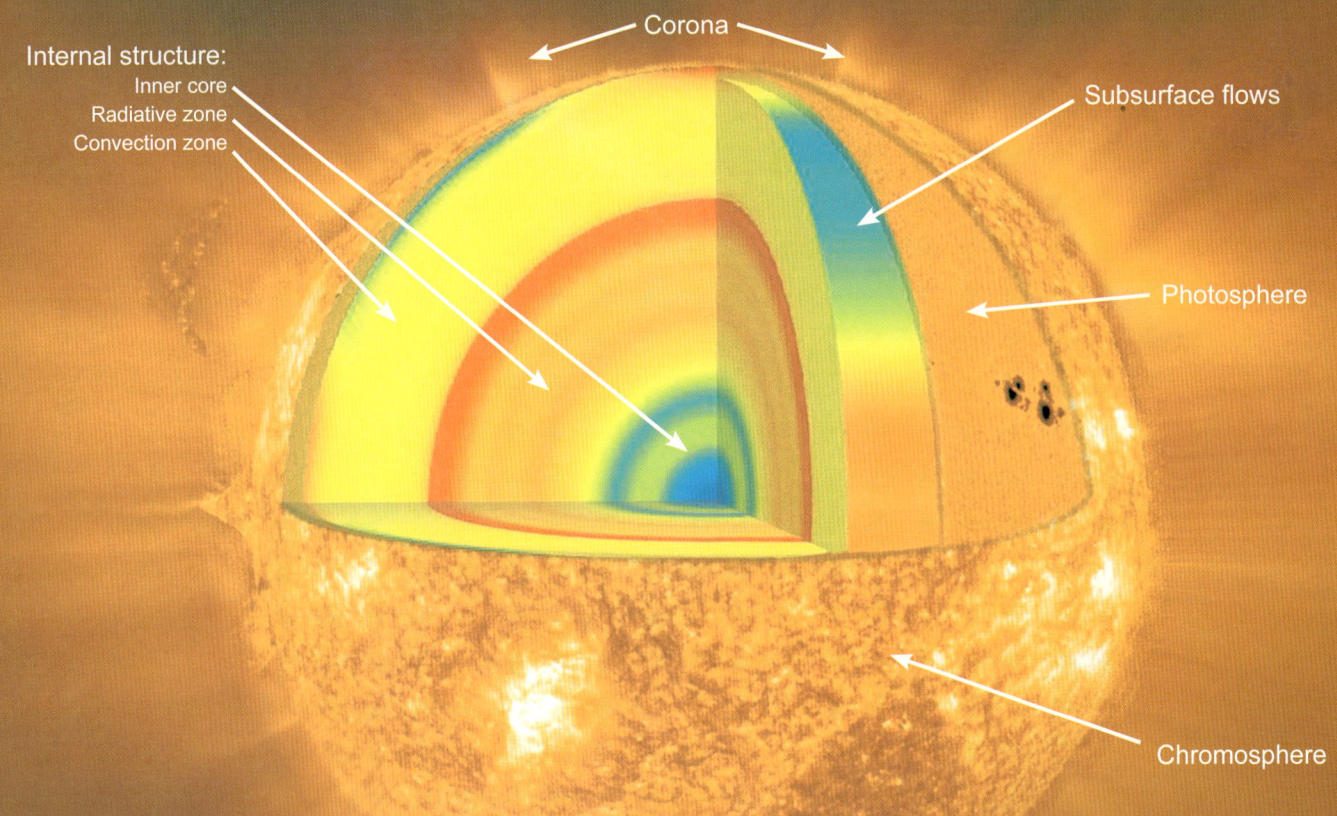

The sun is the closest star to Earth, at a mean distance from our planet of 149.60 million km. This distance is known as an Astronomical Unit (abbreviated AU), and sets the scale for measuring distances all across our solar system.

The sun is held together by gravitational attraction producing immense pressure and temperature at its core. The sun has six regions—the core, the radiative zone, and the convective zone in the interior; the visible surface, the photosphere; the chromosphere; and the outermost region, the corona.

At the **core**, the temperature is about 15 million degree Celsius, which is sufficient to sustain thermonuclear fusion. The energy produced in the core powers the sun and produces essentially all the heat and light we receive on Earth. Energy from the core is carried outward by radiation, which bounces around the **radiative zone**, taking about 170,000 years to get from the core to the convective zone. The temperature drops below 2 million degree Celsius in the **convective zone**, where large bubbles of hot plasma (a soup of ionized atoms) move upwards.

Astonishing fact

99 per cent of our solar systems mass is concentrated in the sun.

7

The sun's surface, the photosphere is a 500 km thick region, from which most of the sun's radiation escapes outward and is detected as the sunlight we observe here on Earth about eight minutes after it leaves the sun. Sunspots in the photosphere are areas with strong magnetic fields that are cooler and thus darker than the surrounding region. The number of sunspots goes up and down every 11 years as part of the sun's magnetic activity cycle. Also connected to this cycle are bright solar flares and huge coronal mass ejections that blast off the sun.

The temperature of the photosphere is about 5,500 degree Celsius. Above the photosphere lie the tenuous chromosphere and the corona ('crown'). Visible light from these top regions is usually too weak to be seen against the brighter photosphere, but during total solar eclipses, when the Moon covers the photosphere, the chromosphere can be seen as a red rim around the sun while the corona forms a beautiful white crown with plasma streaming outward, forming the points of the crown.

Astonishing fact

The sun is 330,330 times larger than the Earth!

Astonishing fact
For 186 days one cannot see the sun in the North Pole.

The sun's magnetic field

The sun is a magnetically active star. It supports a strong, changing magnetic field that varies year-to-year and reverses direction about every eleven years around solar maximum. The sun's magnetic field leads to many effects that are collectively called solar activity, including sunspots on the surface of the sun, solar flares, and variations in solar wind that carry material through the solar system. Effects of solar activity on Earth include auroras at moderate to high latitudes, and the disruption of radio communications and electric power. Solar activity is thought to have played a large role in the formation and evolution of the solar system.

All matter in the sun is in the form of gas and plasma because of its high temperatures. This makes it possible for the sun to rotate faster at its equator (about 25 days) than it does at higher latitudes (about 35 days near its poles). The differential rotation of the sun's latitudes causes its magnetic field lines to become twisted together over time, causing magnetic field loops to erupt from the sun's surface and trigger the formation of the sun's dramatic sunspots and solar prominences. This twisting action creates the solar dynamo and an 11-year solar cycle of magnetic activity as the sun's magnetic field reverses itself about every 11 years.

The solar magnetic field extends well beyond the sun itself. The magnetized solar wind plasma carries sun's magnetic field into the space forming what is called the **interplanetary magnetic field**.

Characteristics of the sun

Chemical composition

The sun, like most other stars, is made up mostly of atoms of the chemical element hydrogen. The second most plentiful element in the sun is helium and almost all the remaining matter consists of atoms of seven other elements. For every 1 million atoms of hydrogen in the entire sun, there are 98,000 atoms of helium, 850 of oxygen, 360 of carbon, 120 of neon, 110 of nitrogen, 40 of magnesium, 35 of iron, and 35 of silicon. So about 94 per cent of the atoms are hydrogen, and 0.1 per cent are elements other than hydrogen and helium.

But hydrogen is the lightest of all elements, and so it accounts for only about 72 per cent of the mass. Helium makes up around 26 per cent.

The inside of the sun and most of its atmosphere consist of plasma. Plasma is basically a gas whose temperature has been raised to such a high level that it becomes sensitive to magnetism. Scientists sometimes emphasize the difference in behaviour between plasma and other gases. They say that plasma is a fourth state of matter, alongside solid, liquid and gas.

Astonishing fact

Twice during Mercury's orbit, it gets so close to the sun and speeds so much that the sun seems to go backwards in the sky.

Characteristics of the sun

Size

The sun is 1,390,000 km in diameter that compares with 12,756 km for diameter of the Earth. In other words, the diameter of the sun is over 100 times the diameter of the Earth. This is equal to 109 Earth diameters and almost 10 times the size of the largest planet, Jupiter. All of the planets orbit the sun because of its enormous gravity. It has about 333,000 times the Earth's mass and is over 1,000 times as massive as Jupiter. It has so much mass that it is able to produce its own light. This feature is what distinguishes stars from planets.

Mass

The mass of the sun is about 2×10^{30} kg (2 followed by 30 zeros). It is one of the larger stars in our Milky Way galaxy. The mediam size of stars in our galaxy is less than half the mass of the sun. In comparison, the Earth is 6×10^{24} kg. This means that the mass of the sun is over 300,000 times greater than that of the Earth.

Distance

The sun is 149,600,000 km from the Earth. Since the speed of light is 303,000 km/sec, it takes the light slightly over 8 minutes to get from the sun to the Earth.

The distance of the sun to the Earth is called an Astronomical Unit (AU) and is sometimes used to denote large distances that are less than a light year.

Astonishing fact

If the sun were the size of a beach ball then Jupiter would be the size of a golf ball and the Earth would be as small as a pea!

SUN

Rotation

The sun rotates on its axis, which is approximately the same axis that most of the planets revolved around the sun. Since the sun is primarily made of very hot gas, the surface at the equator rotates once every 25.4 days. The rotation near the poles takes around 36 days. Also the surface swirls in high and low pressure areas, similar to those that occurs on Earth.

Temperature

Its temperature is extremely hot, with the surface being about 5000 degree Celsius and the centre core at 15,600,000 degree Celsius. The high temperature of the core, along with extreme pressure from the sun's mass, result in nuclear fusion reactions.

Radiation

The energy released from the fusion reactions near the sun's core is in the form of very high frequency electromagnetic waves called gamma rays.

As this radiation moves towards the sun's surface, it is absorbed by atoms in the sun's interior. After absorption, the rays are then re-emitted at lower frequencies. This process continues until the radiation reaches the sun's surface. By that time it is primarily visible light.

Astonishing fact

A comet's tail begins to melt as it nears the sun. A vast plume of gas millions of km across is blown out behind by the solar wind. The tail is what you see, shining as the sunlight catches it.

Characteristics of the sun

Energy output

Most of the energy emitted by the sun is visible light and a related form of radiation known as infrared rays, which we feel as heat. Visible light and infrared rays are two forms of electromagnetic radiation. The sun also emits particle radiation, made up mostly of protons and electrons.

Colour

In popular culture, the sun is yellow. But the colour of the sun is actually white. It's only when light from the sun passes through the Earth's atmosphere that it changes in colour, from white to yellow.

> ## Astonishing fact
> Hipparchus was the first astronomer to try to work out and see how far away the sun actually is.

The atmosphere of the Earth scatters sunlight, removing the shorter wavelength light – blue and violet. Once you reduce those colours from the spectrum of light coming from the sun, it appears more yellow. But if you could fly up and see the sun from space, the colour of the sun would be pure white.

SUN

Astonishing fact

The luminosity of the sun is equivalent to the luminosity of 4 trillion trillion light bulbs of 100 watt!

Features

Solar flares

A solar flare is a thunderous explosion that occurs in the solar corona and chromosphere within the atmosphere of the sun. The incredible energy level of a solar flare is equivalent to tens of millions of atomic bombs exploding at the same time!

Solar flares were first known to be occurring in 1859. Solar flare activity can vary from several per day to only a few a month, depending mostly upon the overall activity of the sun as a whole. Solar activity generally varies on an 11-year cycle. At the peak of this 'solar cycle' there are typically more sunspots on the surface of the sun, which ultimately leads to more frequently occurring solar flares.

Solar flares are typically classified as A, B, C, M or X, depending upon the degree of their peak flux. Most solar flares occur in or around sun spots as the result of intense magnetic fields emerging from the sun's surface into the corona. The powerful energy commonly associated with solar flares can take as long as several days to build up, but only minutes to release.

Solar wind

Solar wind is a continuous stream of matter that flows outward from the sun in all directions. The solar wind is composed of electrically charged particles primarily electrons and the nuclei of hydrogen and helium atoms. The particles travel away from the sun at speeds of 320 to 960 km/sec. Relatively few of the particles reach the Earth's atmosphere because the Earth's magnetic field acts as a barrier. Increases in the intensity of the solar wind are associated with auroras, magnetic storms, and other disturbances in the Earth's magnetic field and atmosphere.

It takes the solar wind about 4.5 days to reach Earth; it has a velocity of about 400 km/sec. Since the particles are emitted from the sun as the sun rotates, the solar wind blows in a pinwheel pattern through the solar system. The solar wind affects the entire solar system, including buffeting comets' tails away from the sun, causing auroras on Earth (and some other planets), the disruption of electronic communications on Earth, pushing spacecraft around, etc.

Astonishing fact

The amount of energy reaching the Earth's surface from the sun is 6,000 times the amount of energy used by all human beings worldwide.

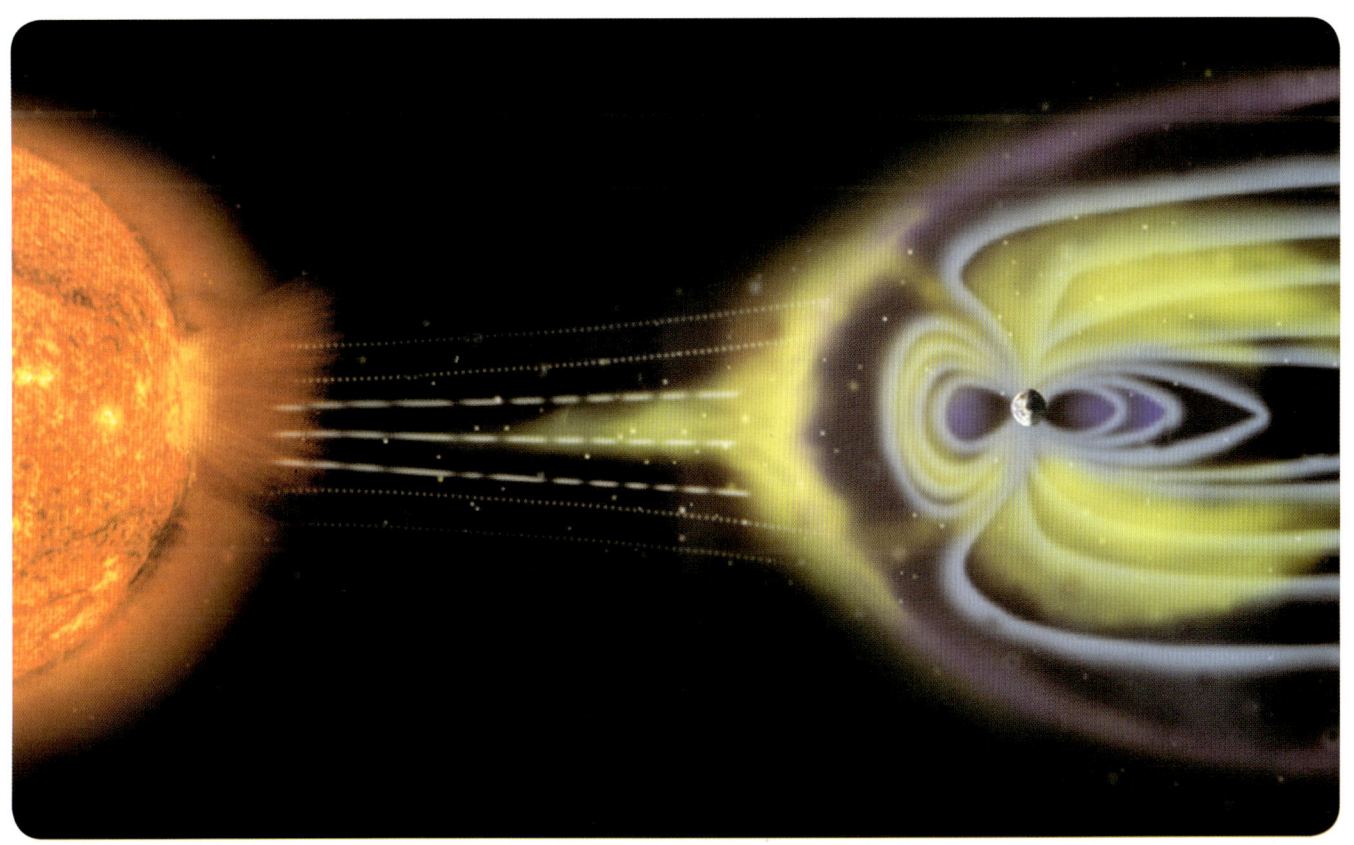

Solar prominence

A solar prominence is an arc of gas that erupts from the surface of the sun. It is often shaped as a loop and although actually very large, cannot be seen without the aid of a strong telescope and some filters. Prominences can loop hundreds and thousands of miles into space. Prominences are held above the sun's surface by strong magnetic fields and can last for many months. At some time in their existence, most prominences will erupt, spewing enormous amounts of solar material into space. The largest ever to be observed was estimated to be 350,000 km long. That's nearly ten times the entire circumference of the Earth!

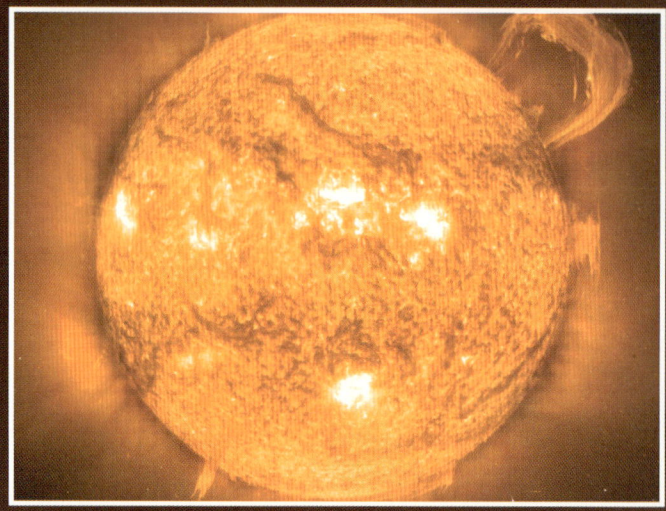

move along the sun's magnetic field lines and increase in temperature up to tens of millions of degrees. These bursts release up to 100 billion kg of plasma. CME's can disrupt Earth's satellites. CME's usually happen independently, but are sometimes associated with solar flares.

Astonishing fact

In Spitsbergen, Norway, at one time of the year the sun shines continuously for three and a half months.

Coronal mass ejections

Coronal mass ejections (abbreviated CME's) are huge, balloon-shaped plasma bursts that come from the sun. As these bursts of solar wind rise above the sun's corona, they

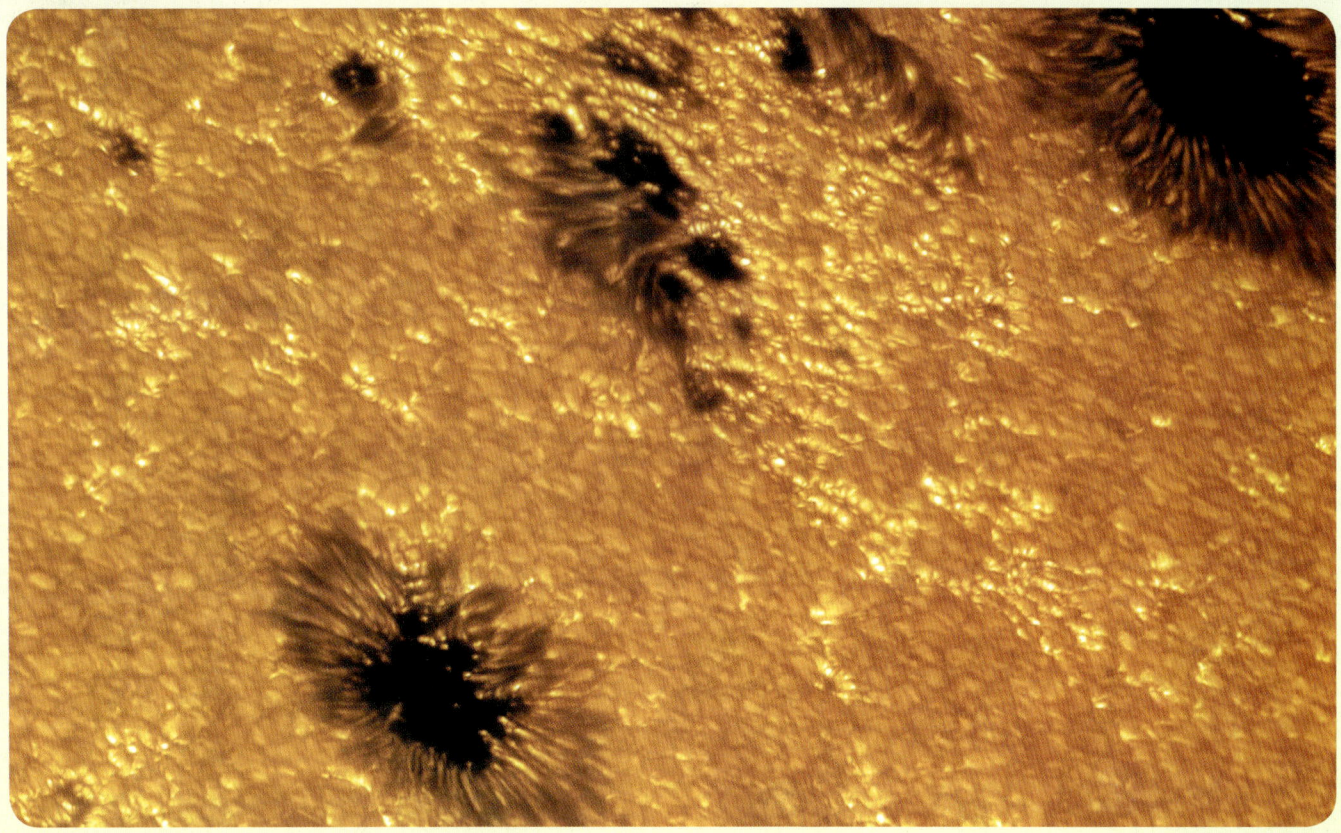

Sunspots

Sunspots appear as dark spots on the visible surface of the sun. Temperatures in the dark centres of sunspots drop to about 3700 K (compared to 5700 K for the surrounding photosphere). They typically last for several days, although very large ones may live for several weeks. Sunspots are magnetic regions on the sun with magnetic field strengths thousands of times stronger than the Earth's magnetic field. Sunspots usually come in groups with two sets of spots. One set has positive or north magnetic field while the other set has negative or south magnetic field. The field is strongest in the darker parts of the sunspots— the umbra. The field is weaker and more horizontal in the lighter part— the penumbra. The largest sunspot ever recorded was visible in March and April 1947 and covered an area of over 18,000 million square km; about a hundred Earths could be fitted into this area!

Sunspot activity occurs as part of an 11-year cycle called the solar cycle where there are periods of maximum and minimum activity.

Astonishing fact

An area on the sun's surface of the size of a postage stamp shines with a power of 1,500,000 candles!

Solar eclipse

A solar eclipse occurs when the moon, during its monthly trip around the Earth, happens to line up exactly between the Earth and the sun, so that it casts a shadow on the Earth. But because of the sun's large diameter, the shadow consists of two regions. The innermost cone of total darkness is called the umbra (Latin for 'shadow'), and it is projected in the centre. Anyone in this central area will observe the total eclipse, because the sun will be temporarily obscured by the moon. The outer shadow is partially illuminated by the sun and is called the penumbra. Anyone in this region will see the partial eclipse, since the sun is only partially obscured by the moon.

The glory of a solar eclipse comes from the dramatic view of the sun's corona or outer atmosphere, which we can see only when the brilliant solar disc is blocked by the moon. The corona is not just light shining from around the disk. It is actually the outermost layer of the solar atmosphere. Although, the gas is very sparse, it is extraordinarily hot (800,000 to 3,000,000 K), even hotter than the surface of the sun! The corona shows up as pearly white streamers and their shape is determined by the sun's current magnetic fields. Thus every eclipse will be unique and beautiful in its own way.

Astonishing fact

The energy being emitted from 1 square cm of the sun's surface is enough to burn 64 light bulbs of 100 watt.

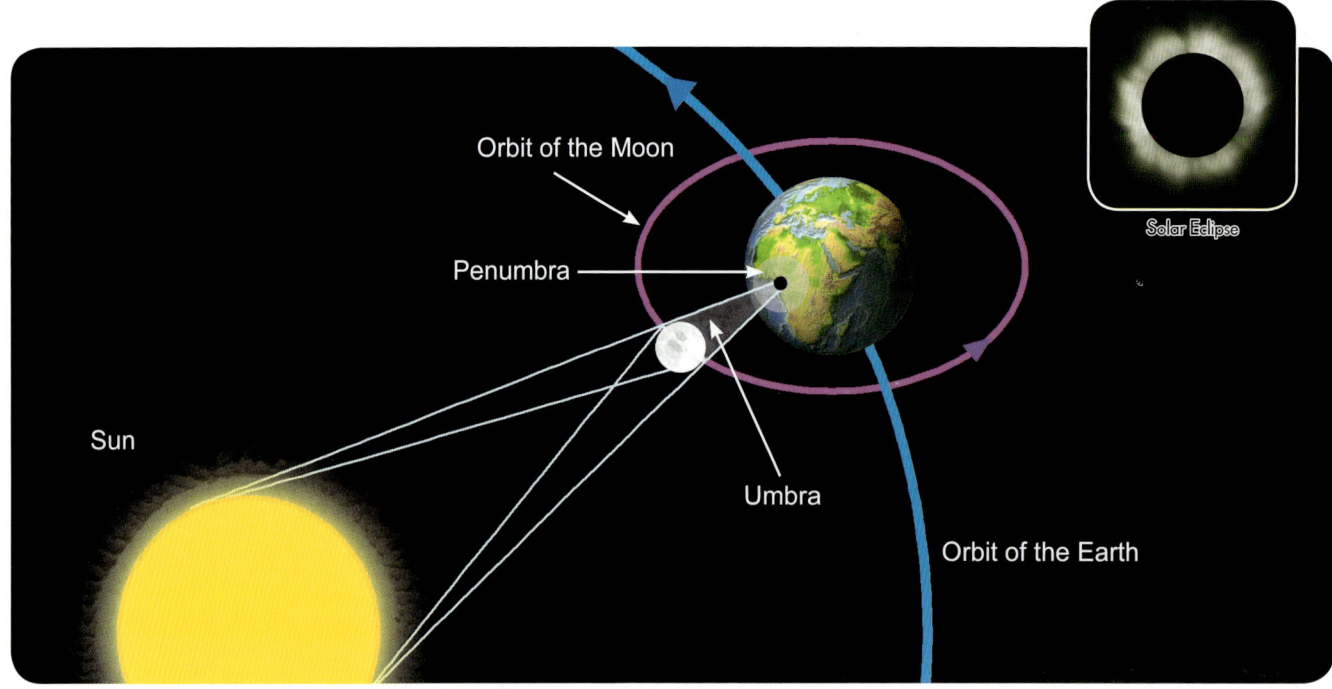

Solar eclipse

Astonishing fact
The light from the sun takes 5.5 hours to travel to Pluto.

Sunlight

Sunlight is the general term for all of the electromagnetic radiation emitted by the sun. Although we see the sun with our eyes in the visible spectrum, the sun is actually releasing everything from radio waves and infrared to ultraviolet and even X-ray radiation. Satellites in orbit estimate that the total amount of sunlight that reaches Earth is about 1.366 kilowatts per square metre.

The Earth is located at an average distance of about 150 million km from the sun. It takes sunlight about 8.3 minutes to cross this distance and reach the Earth. When the sunlight reaches Earth, it's partly absorbed by the Earth's atmosphere. Whatever reaches the ground helps to warm the Earth, and keep it hospitable for life.

The amount of sunlight that the Earth receives changes over the course of the year. This is because the Earth orbits the sun in an elliptical orbit. At its closest point, the Earth actually receives 1.413 kW/m^2, and then at the most distant point of its orbit, the Earth only receives 1.321 kW/m^2.

Planets further away from the sun receive less sunlight. Mars only gets about 550 kW/m^2, while Neptune only receives 1.5 kW/m^2.

SUN

Sunlight is Earth's primary source of energy. The solar constant is the amount of power that the sun deposits per unit area that is directly exposed to sunlight. The solar constant is equal to approximately 1,368 W/m^2 at a distance of one astronomical unit (AU) from the sun (that is, on or near Earth). Sunlight on the surface of Earth is attenuated by the Earth's atmosphere so that less power arrives at the surface—closer to 1,000 W/m^2 in clear conditions when the sun is near the zenith.

Solar energy can be harnessed by a variety of natural and synthetic processes—photosynthesis by plants captures the energy of sunlight and converts it to chemical form (oxygen and reduced carbon compounds), while direct heating or electrical conversion by solar cells are used by solar power equipment to generate electricity or to do other useful work. The energy stored in petroleum and other fossil fuels was originally converted from sunlight by photosynthesis in the distant past.

Astonishing fact

The total amount of fossil fuel used by humans since the first civilization is equivalent to less than 30 days of energy reaching the Earth's surface from sun.

Sunrise and sunset

Although, it looks like the sun is moving through the sky from our vantage point, it's actually the Earth's rotation on its axis that causes the apparent motion of the sun. And that's why we have sunrise and sunset.

Astronomers consider sunrise to be the moment when the leading edge of the sun first peeks up over the horizon in the east. Sunset happens when the sun's trailing edge completely disappears over the horizon in the west.

The sunrise and the sunset times are different for every place on the Earth. It depends on your day of the year, your distance from the equator, and your position within the time zone. That's why sunrise sunset times can be a few minutes different from other locations.

When the sun is just setting or rising, we see it passing through the largest amount of the Earth's atmosphere. As the light passes through this larger amount of atmosphere, the red and orange portions of the light scatter more easily when they encounter particles in the atmosphere. This is why sunrise and sunset can be spectacular, with the beautiful orange and red colours in the sky.

Astonishing fact

The sun is one among the 6000 stars which is visible to the naked eye from the Earth.

Sun's orbit

Astronomers have calculated that it takes the sun 226 million years to completely orbit around the centre of the Milky Way. In other words, that last time that the sun was in its current position in space around the Milky Way, dinosaurs ruled the Earth. In fact, this sun orbit has only happened 20.4 times since the sun itself formed 4.6 billion years ago.

Since the sun is 26,000 light-years from the centre of the Milky Way, it has to travel at an astonishing speed of 782,000 km/h in a circular orbit around the Milky Way centre. Just for comparison, the Earth is rotating at a speed of 1,770 km/h and it is moving at a speed of 108,000 km/h around the sun.

It's estimated that the sun will continue fusing hydrogen for another 7 billon years or so. In other words, it only has another 31 orbits it can make before it runs out of fuel.

Astonishing fact

If a drop sized matter from the core of the sun is placed on the surface of the Earth, no living organism will survive for a distance of 150 km from that drop.

Sun's orbit

Astonishing fact

The surface area of sun is equivalent to that of 11,990 Earths!

Solar space missions

Astronomers study the sun using special instruments. Scientists analyze how and why the amount of light from the sun varies over time, the effect of the sun's light on the Earth's climate, spectral lines, the sun's magnetic field, the solar wind, and many other solar phenomena. The outer regions of the sun (the corona) are studied during solar eclipses.

The first satellites designed to observe the sun were NASA's Pioneers 5, 6, 7, 8 and 9, which were launched between 1959 and 1968. These probes orbited the sun at a distance similar to that of the Earth, and made the first detailed measurements of the solar wind and the solar magnetic field. Pioneer 9 operated for a particularly long time, transmitting data until May 1983.

In the 1970s, two Helios spacecraft and the Skylab Apollo Telescope Mount provided scientists with significant new data on solar wind and the solar corona. The Helios 1 and 2 probes studied the solar wind from an orbit carrying the spacecraft inside Mercury's orbit at perihelion.

In 1980, the Solar Maximum Mission was launched by NASA. This spacecraft was designed to observe gamma rays, X-rays and UV radiation from solar flares during a time of high solar activity and solar luminosity. The Solar Maximum Mission subsequently acquired thousands of images of the solar corona before re-entering the Earth's atmosphere in June 1989.

23

SUN

Launched in 1991, Japan's Yohkoh (sunbeam) satellite observed solar flares at X-ray wavelengths. Yohkoh observed an entire solar cycle but went into standby mode when an annular eclipse in 2001 caused it to lose its lock on the sun. It was destroyed by atmospheric re-entry in 2005.

One of the most important solar missions till date has been the Solar and Heliospheric Observatory (SOHO), jointly built by the European Space Agency and NASA and launched on 2 December, 1995. It has proven to be so useful that a follow-on mission, the Solar Dynamics Observatory was launched in February, 2010. Situated at the **Lagrangian point** between the Earth and the sun (at which the gravitational pull from both is equal), SOHO has provided a constant view of the sun at many wavelengths since its launch. Besides its direct solar observation, SOHO has enabled the discovery of a large number of comets, mostly very tiny sun grazing comets which incinerate as they pass the sun.

Astonishing fact

The volume of sun is equivalent to the volume of 1.3 million Earths.

Solar space missions

All these satellites have observed the sun from the plane of the ecliptic, and so have only observed its equatorial regions in detail. The Ulysses probe was launched in 1990 to study the sun's Polar Regions. Once Ulysses was in its scheduled orbit, it began observing the solar wind and magnetic field strength at high solar latitudes, finding that the solar wind from high latitudes was moving at about 750 km/s which were slower than expected, and that there were large magnetic waves emerging from high latitudes which scattered galactic cosmic rays.

Elemental abundances in the photosphere are well-known from spectroscopic studies, but the composition of the interior of the sun is more poorly understood. A solar wind sample return mission, Genesis, was designed to allow astronomers to directly measure the composition of solar material. Genesis returned to Earth in 2004 but was damaged by a crash landing after its parachute failed to deploy on re-entry into Earth's atmosphere. Despite severe damage, some usable samples have been recovered from the spacecraft's sample return module and are undergoing analysis.

The Solar Terrestrial Relations Observatory (STEREO) mission was launched in October 2006. Two identical spacecrafts were launched into orbits that caused them to (respectively) pull further ahead of and fall gradually behind the Earth. This enabled stereoscopic imaging of the sun and solar phenomena, such as coronal mass ejections.

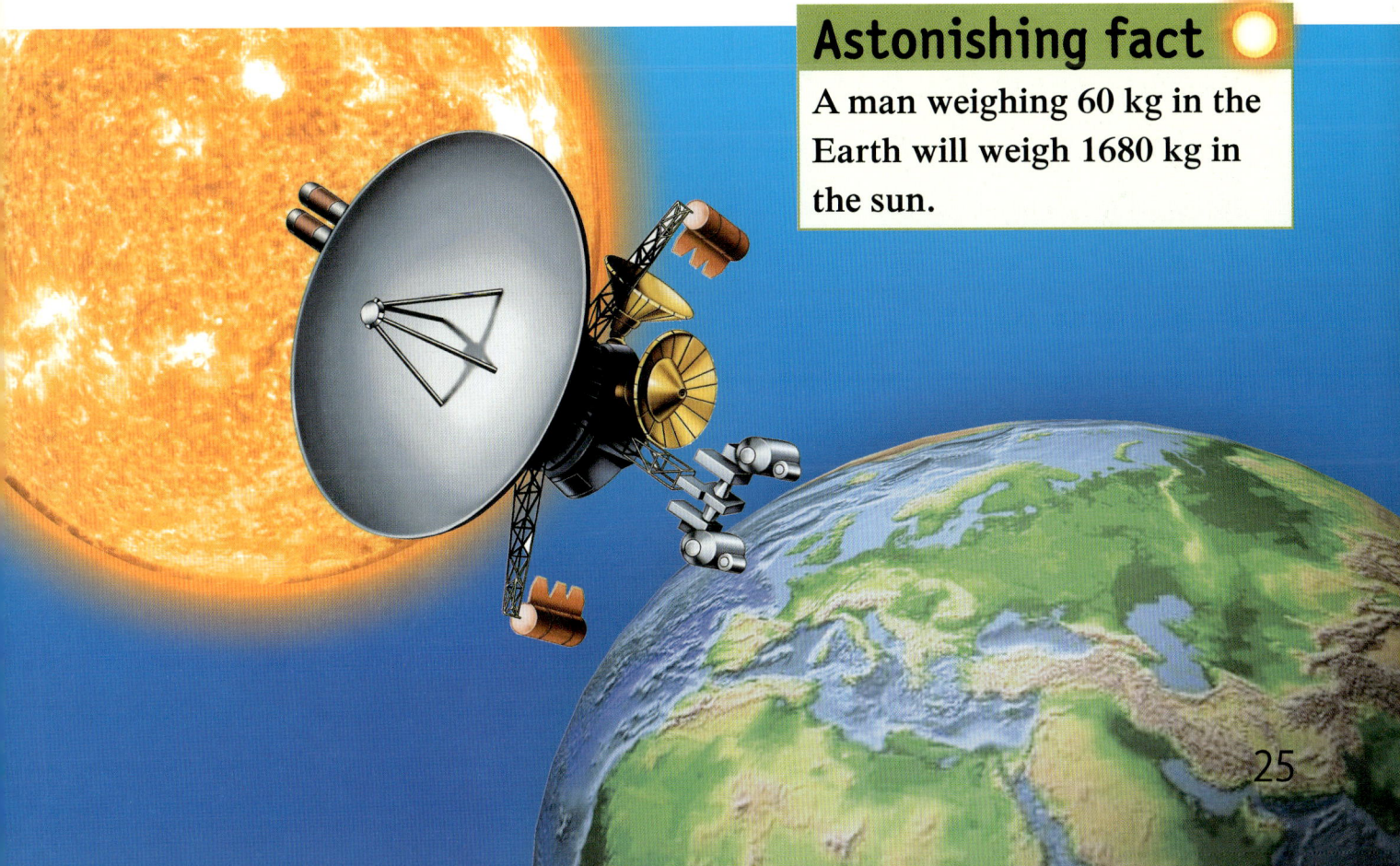

Astonishing fact

A man weighing 60 kg in the Earth will weigh 1680 kg in the sun.

Sun in culture

The sun is the star at the centre of the solar system and all the planets orbit around it. Most life on Earth evolved with the sun in mind; the rising and setting sun defined the cycle of daily life. Ancient peoples were entirely dependent on the sun for light; only the light from a full moon gave any way to see in the night. It wasn't until the invention of fire that humans had any way to get any work done after the sun went down.

Since the sun was such an important object, many ancient people treated it with reverence and considered the sun a god. Many worshipped the sun, and built monuments to celebrate it. Monuments like Stonehenge in England, and the Pyramids of Egypt were used to mark the position of the sun over the course of the year.

It was long thought that the sun orbited around the Earth, but it was Nicolaus Copernicus who first proposed a sun-centered Solar System. This theory gained evidence from Galileo and other early astronomers. By the 1800s, solar astronomy was very advanced, with astronomers carefully tracking sunspots, measuring absorption lines in the spectrum of light from the sun, and discovering infrared.

> Proxima Centauri is the closest star around the sun, at a distance of 4.3 light years.

Sun in culture

> **Astonishing fact**
>
> The sun is orbited by nine major planets— Mercury, Venus, Earth, Mars, Jupiter, Saturn, Uranus, Neptune, and Pluto (no longer an official planet).

Humans have long recognized the sun's role in supporting life on Earth, and as a result many societies throughout history have paid homage to the sun by giving it prominent roles in their religions and mythologies.

The sun is sometimes referred to by its Latin name **Sol** or by its Greek name **Helios**. Its astrological and astronomical symbol is a circle with a point at its centre. The ancient Greeks grouped the sun together with the other celestial bodies which moved across the sky, calling them all planets.

The religious significance of the sun has its roots in the very earliest of recorded Western history. Both the ancient Greeks and ancient Romans worshipped one or more solar deities.

Many Greek myths personify the sun as a Titan named Helios, who wore a shining crown and rode a chariot across the sky, causing day. The Roman Empire adopted Helios into their own mythology and changed its name to Sol. The title Sol Invictus ('the undefeated sun') was applied to several solar deities and depicted on several types of Roman coins during the 3rd and 4th centuries.

SUN

Sun god Ra

The sun was also worshipped in many pre-Columbian societies in the Americas, including the Incas and the Aztecs.

The worship of the sun in the Eastern world has its historical origin in Ancient Egypt. The Egyptians identified the sun with **Ra**, one of the major deities in their religion.

In Hindu religious literature, the sun is notably mentioned as the visible form of God that one can see every day. In Hinduism, **Surya** is the chief solar deity. Many scripts from Hindu mythology referred the sun as a King, who rides on a chariot of seven horses (this is indication of seven colours from sunlight).

In the Quran, the Islamic religious scripture, the sun like other celestial objects is not endowed with any particular religious significance or symbolic meaning. Due to the widespread presence of sun-worshiping cults in Pre-Islamic Arabia, Muslim doctrine, the Shariah forbade all prayers during the rising and setting of the sun, to symbolically refute its divinity.

Pre-Islamic Arab pagans considered solar eclipses and other celestial occurrences as omens signalling the passing of an important figure or other Earthly events. However, this belief was refuted explicitly by Prophet Muhammad in the year 632 C.E, when the death of his son coincided with a solar eclipse: 'The sun and the Moon are from among the evidences of God. They do not eclipse because of someone's death or life.'

Unlike the Earth, the sun is completely gaseous; there is no solid surface on the sun.

Surya

The fate of the sun

The sun has been shining for about 4.5 billion years. The size of the sun is a balance between the outward pressure made by the release of energy from nuclear fusion and the inward pull of gravity. Over its 4.5 billion years of life, the sun's radius has increased about 6 per cent bigger. It has enough hydrogen fuel to burn for about 10 billion years, meaning it has a bit over 5 billion years left, and during this time it will continue to expand at the same rate.

When the core runs out of hydrogen fuel, it will contract under the weight of gravity. However, some hydrogen fusion will occur in the upper layers. As the core contracts, it heats up and this heats the upper layers causing them to expand. As the outer layers expand, the radius of the sun will increase and it will become a **red giant**, an elderly star.

The radius of the red giant sun will be 100 times of what it is now, lying just beyond the Earth's orbit, so the Earth will plunge into the core of the red giant sun and be vapourised. At some point after this, the core will become hot enough to cause the helium to fuse into carbon.

When the helium fuel will be exhausted, the core will expand and cool. The upper layers will expand and

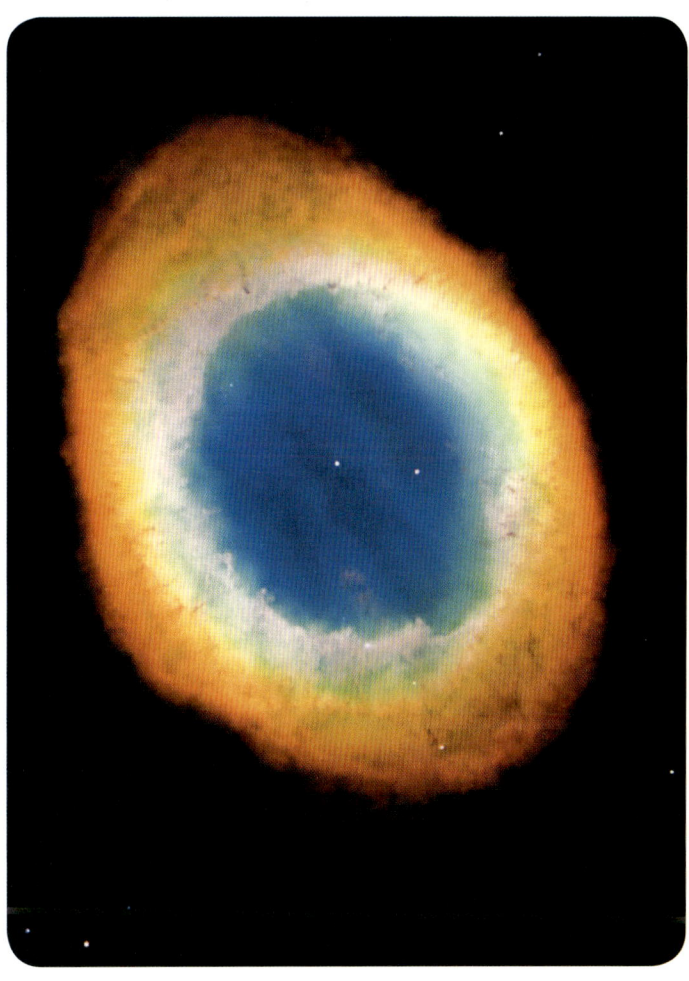

eject material. Finally, the core will cool into a **white dwarf**.

Eventually, it will further cool into a nearly invisible **black dwarf**. This entire process will take a few billion years.

Astonishing fact

100,000,000,000 tons of dynamite would have to be detonated every second to match the energy produced by the sun.

Astonishing fact

In ancient Egypt, the sun God Ra was the dominant figure among the high gods. He achieved the highest status because he was believed to have created himself and eight other gods.

What the sun does for us

The sun keeps us in place. Even though the Earth is located approximately 140 million km away from the sun, the sun's gravity can reach out and hang onto us. Without this pull of gravity, we would just fly off into space, away from the warmth and light of the sun, and out into the cold black of space. This is a very important job that the sun does for us, and makes everything else possible.

The sun helps with the tides. Most of the daily ocean tides happen because of the moon. But we experience our highest and lowest tides when the sun, Earth and moon are lined up in a row.

The sun causes the weather. The sun is constantly heating up the planet. But it's not always heating the same parts of the planet at the same time. It's these differences that create the weather. When one part of the Earth is warm like the land, and another part is cold like the oceans, air moves from one region to the other creating winds. When the sun heats water, it evaporates, becoming clouds and eventually falls again as rain. We wouldn't have weather without the sun.

The sun gives us energy. In addition to the heat we receive from the sun, plants absorb energy from the sun, mix this with carbon dioxide in the atmosphere, and grow. All of the fossil fuels we use to run our modern economy come from energy from the sun, stored over millions of years.

Test Your MEMORY

1. What is the sun?

2. Write briefly about the formation of the sun.

3. Write about the layers of the sun.

4. Write about the sun's magnetic field.

5. Write two characteristics of the sun.

6. What are sunspots?

7. What is a solar eclipse?

8. What is sunlight?

9. Write briefly about the sun's orbit?

10. Write about the solar space missions.

11. How is the sun portrayed in various culture?

12. What is the fate of the sun?

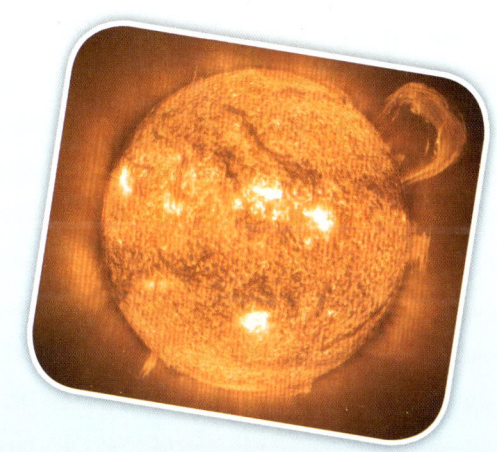

Index

A

asteroids 3
astronomers 5, 6, 21, 22, 23, 25, 26
Astronomical Unit (AU) 7, 11, 20

C

carbon 10, 29, 30
chromosphere 7, 8, 14
comets 3, 15, 24
convective zone 7
core 7, 12, 22, 29
corona 7, 8, 14, 16, 18, 23
coronal mass ejections 4, 8, 16, 25

E

electromagnetic radiation 13, 19
electromagnetic waves 12
electrons 13, 15

G

gamma rays 12, 23

H

helium 3, 5, 10, 15, 29

hydrogen 3, 5, 6, 10, 15, 22, 29

I

infrared rays 13
iron 10
interplanetary magnetic field 9

L

light year 11

M

magnesium 10
meteoroids 3
milky way 4, 11, 22

N

neon 10
nitrogen 10

O

oxygen 10, 20

P

particle radiation 13
penumbra 17, 18
photosphere 7, 8, 17, 25
photosynthesis 3, 20
plasma 10

protons 13

R

radiation 7, 8, 12, 13, 19, 23
radiative zone 7

S

silicon 10
sol 27
solar eclipse 18, 28, 31
solar energy 20
solar flare 14
solar flares 4, 8, 9, 14, 16, 23, 24
solar prominence 16
solar wind 15
spectrum of light 13, 26
sunspots 8, 17
solar constant 20

U

umbra 17, 18

… PEGASUS ENCYCLOPEDIA LIBRARY

Space
UNIVERSE

Edited by: Pallabi B. Tomar, Hitesh Iplani
Managing editor: Tapasi De
Designed by: Vijesh Chahal, Anil Kumar, Rohit Kumar
Illustrated by: Suman S. Roy, Tanoy Choudhury
Colouring done by: Vinay Kumar, Kiran Kumari & Pradeep Kumar

CONTENTS

What is Universe?... 3

Origin of the Universe 5

The composition of the Universe 8

Parts of the Universe 10

Black Holes, Pulsars and Quasars 17

Age of the Universe 23

Size of the Universe 24

Shape of the Universe 26

Evolution of life in the Universe 27

Ultimate fate of the Universe 29

Test Your Memory... 31

Index..32

What is Universe?

The Universe is a huge wide-open space that holds everything from the smallest particle to the biggest galaxy. No one knows just how big the Universe is. Astronomers try to measure it all the time. They use a special instrument called a **spectroscope** to tell whether an object is moving away from Earth or towards the Earth. Based on the information from this instrument, scientists have learned that the Universe is still growing outwards in every direction.

Scientists believe that about 13.7 billion years ago, a powerful explosion called the **Big Bang** happened. This powerful explosion set the Universe into motion and this motion continues even today. Scientists are not yet sure if the motion will stop, change direction or keep going forever.

Scientists believe that hydrogen comprises approximately 90 to 99 per cent of all matter in the Universe.

UNIVERSE

Many cultures have stories describing the origin of the world, which maybe roughly grouped into common types. In one type of story, the world is born from a world egg; such stories include the Finnish epic poem **Kalevala**, the Chinese story of Pangu or the Indian **Brahmanda Purana**. In the related stories, the creation idea is caused by a single entity emanating or producing something by himself or herself, as in the Tibetan Buddhism concept of Adi-Buddha, the ancient Greek story of Gaia (Mother Earth), the Aztec Goddess Coatlicue myth or the ancient Egyptian God Atum story. In another type of story, the world is created from the union of male and female deities, as in the Maori story of Rangi and Papa. In other stories, the Universe is created by crafting it from pre-existing materials, such as the corpse of a dead god — as from Tiamat in the Babylonian epic Enuma Elish or from the giant Ymir in Norse mythology. In other stories, the Universe emanates from fundamental principles, such as Brahman and Prakrti or the yin and yang of the Tao.

A space vehicle must move at a rate of 11 km per second to escape the Earth's gravitational pull.

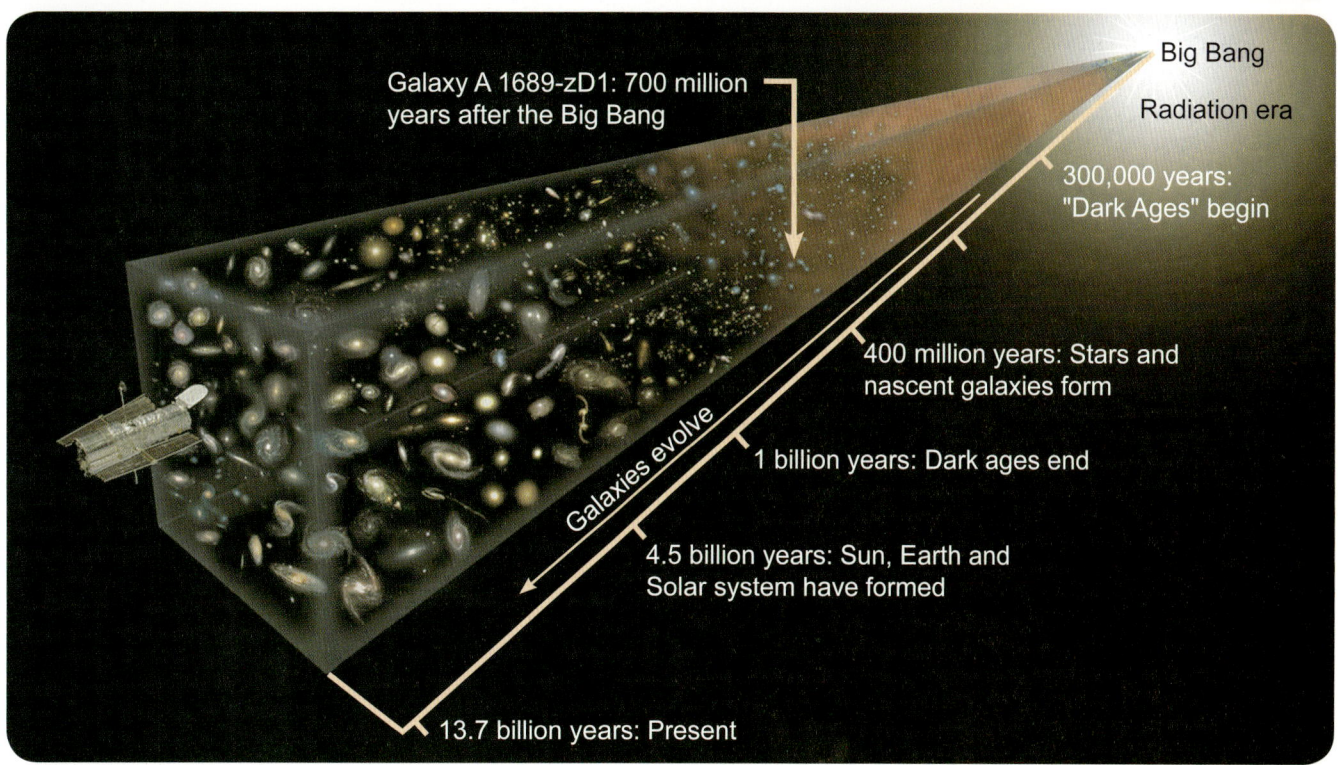

Origin of the Universe

Most astronomers believe that the Universe began in a Big Bang about 14 billion years ago. At that time, the entire Universe was inside a bubble that was thousands of times smaller than a pinhead. It was hotter and denser than anything we can imagine.

Then it suddenly exploded. The Universe that we know was born. Time, space and matter all began with the Big Bang. In a fraction of a second, the Universe grew from smaller than a single atom to bigger than a galaxy. And it kept on growing at a fantastic rate. It is still expanding.

As the Universe expanded and cooled, energy changed into particles of matter and antimatter. These two opposite types of particles largely destroyed each other. But some matter survived. More stable particles called **protons** and **neutrons** started to form when the Universe was one second old.

Over the next three minutes, the temperature dropped below 1 billion degrees Celsius. It was now cool enough for the protons and neutrons to come together, forming hydrogen and helium nuclei.

After 300000 years, the Universe had cooled to about 3000 degrees. Atomic nuclei could finally capture electrons to form atoms. The Universe was filled with clouds of hydrogen and helium gas.

UNIVERSE

The origin of the Big Bang theory can be credited to Edwin Hubble. Hubble made the observation that the Universe is continuously expanding. He discovered that a galaxie's velocity is proportional to its distance. Galaxies that are twice as far from us move twice as fast. Another consequence is that the Universe is expanding in every direction. This observation means that it has taken every galaxy the same amount of time to move from a common starting position to its current position. Just as the Big Bang provided for the foundation of the Universe, Hubble's observations provided for the foundation of the Big Bang theory.

Since the Big Bang, the Universe has been continuously expanding and, thus, there has been more and more distance between clusters of galaxies. This phenomenon of galaxies moving farther away from each other is known as the **red shift**. As light from distant galaxies approach Earth, there is an increase of space between Earth and the galaxy, which leads to wavelengths being stretched.

> Halley's Comet is seen after every 76 years in the sky. It was last seen in the year 1986.

6

Origin of the Universe

In addition to the understanding of the velocity of galaxies emanating from a single point, there is further evidence for the Big Bang. In 1964, two astronomers, Arno Penzias and Robert Wilson, in an attempt to detect microwaves from outer space, inadvertently discovered a noise of extraterrestrial origin. The noise did not seem to emanate from one location but instead, it came from all directions at once. It became obvious that what they heard was radiation from the farthest reaches of the Universe which had been left over from the Big Bang. This discovery of the radioactive aftermath of the initial explosion lent much credence to the Big Bang theory.

The Big Bang theory provides a viable solution to one of the most pressing questions of all times. It is important to understand, however, that the theory itself is constantly being revised. As more observations are made and more research conducted, the Big Bang theory becomes more complete and our knowledge of the origins of the Universe becomes more substantial.

Astonishing fact

More than 75 million meteors enter the Earth's atmosphere everyday; but they disintegrate before hitting the ground.

The composition of the Universe

The chemical composition of the Universe and the physical nature of its constituent matter are topics that have occupied scientists for centuries. All over the Universe stars work as giant reprocessing plants taking light chemical elements and transforming them into heavier ones. The original composition of the Universe is studied in such fine detail because it is one of the keys to our understanding of processes in the very early Universe.

Human beings, the air we breathe, and the distant stars are all made up of protons, neutrons and electrons. Protons and neutrons are bound together into nuclei and atoms are nuclei surrounded by a full complement of electrons. Hydrogen is composed of one proton and one electron. Helium is composed of two protons, two neutrons and two electrons. Carbon is composed of six protons, six neutrons and six electrons. Heavier elements, such as iron, lead and uranium, contain even larger numbers of protons, neutrons and electrons. Astronomers like to call all material made up of protons, neutrons and electrons '**baryonic matter**'.

Until about thirty years ago, astronomers thought that the Universe was composed almost entirely of this 'baryonic matter', ordinary atoms. However, in the past few decades, there has been ever more evidence accumulating that suggests that there is something in the Universe that we cannot see, perhaps some new form of matter.

The composition of the Universe

According to the latest observational evidence, ordinary matter, including stars, planets, dust and gas, only make up a tiny fraction of the Universe (5 per cent). The rest is the elusive dark matter (25 per cent) and dark energy (70 per cent).

Dark energy: A mysterious (and as yet hypothetical) form of energy which is spread out uniformly throughout space (and time) and which has anti-gravitational properties. It is one of the possible explanations for the current accelerating rate of expansion of the Universe.

Dark matter: Matter is not visible to us because it emits no radiation that we can observe, but it is detectable gravitationally.

Hydrogen & Helium gas: Hydrogen and Helium are the most abundant element in the Universe. This element is found in great abundance in stars and gas giant planets.

Astonishing fact

Saturn's rings are not solid. Although they appear to be thin, Saturn's rings are actually particles of ice, dust and rock. The particles range from the size of a grain of sand to larger than skyscraper buildings!

Stars: A ball of mostly hydrogen and helium gas that shines extremely brightly. Our sun is a star.

Neutrinos: A small particle that has no charge and is thought to have very little mass. Neutrinos are created in energetic collisions between nuclear particles. The Universe is filled with them but they rarely collide with anything.

Heavy elements: Planets like ours.

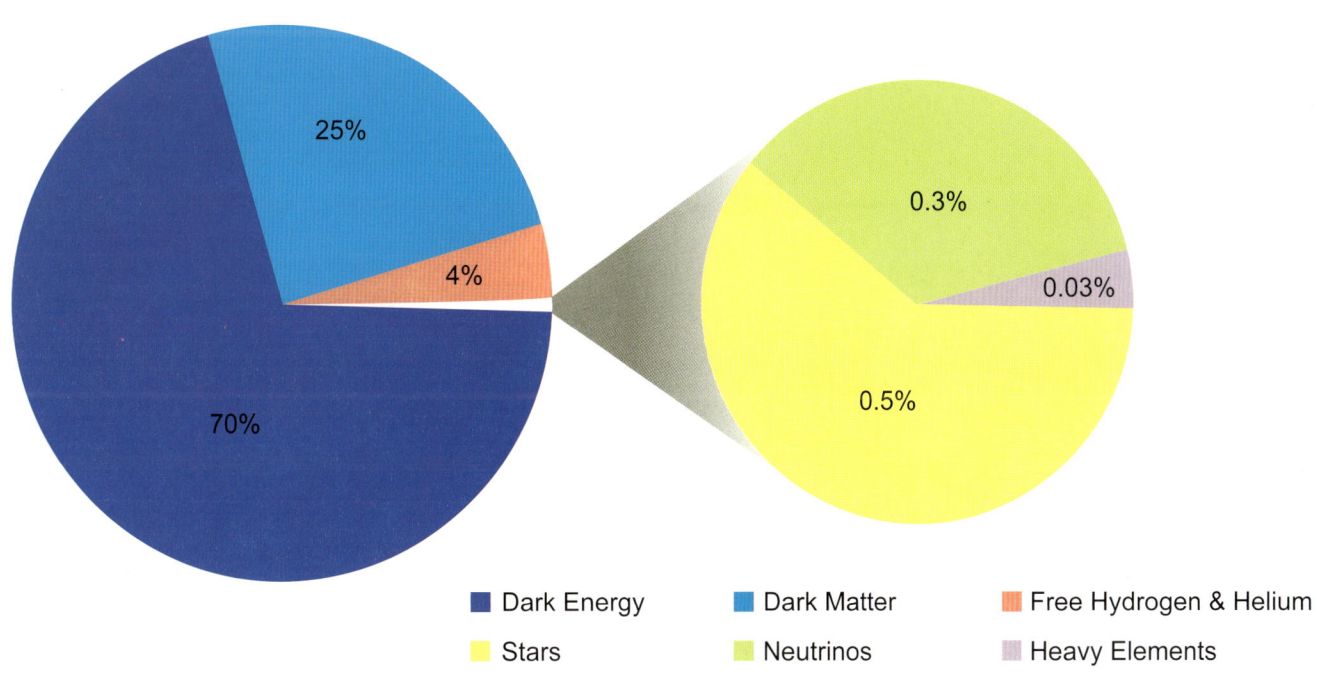

UNIVERSE

Parts of the Universe

Universe is the vast empty space around us and everything that is in it. It contains numerous heavenly bodies like the sun, the planets, moon, stars, meteors and meteorites.

The main constituents of the Universe are:

The solar system, the stars and the galaxies.

The Solar System

The solar system consists of the sun, the nine planets and their satellites, asteroids, comets and meteors.

Sun

The sun is a huge, glowing ball at the centre of our solar system. The sun provides light, heat, and other energy to Earth. The sun is made up entirely of gas. Most of it is a type of gas that is sensitive to magnetism. Nine planets and their moons, tens of thousands of asteroids and trillions of comets revolve around the sun. The sun and all these objects are in the solar system. Earth travels around the sun at an average distance of about 149,600,000 km from it.

Astonishing fact

There are approximately 10,000 pieces of materials revolving around the Earth. About 3,000 of these pieces are satellites, the rest are odd bits of debris.

Parts of the Universe

Planets

Our solar system consists of the sun, eight planets, moons, many dwarf planets (or plutoids), an asteroid belt, comets, meteors, and others. The sun is the centre of our solar system; the planets, their moons, a belt of asteroids, comets and other rocks and gas orbit the sun.

The eight planets that orbit the sun are (in order from the sun): Mercury, Venus, Earth, Mars, Jupiter, Saturn, Uranus, Neptune. Another large body is Pluto, now classified as a dwarf planet or plutoid. A belt of asteroids (minor planets made of rock and metal) lies between Mars and Jupiter. These objects all orbit the sun in roughly circular orbits that lie in the same plane, the ecliptic.

Astonishing fact

There are more stars in the Universe than there are grains of sand on Earth!

The largest planet is Jupiter. It is followed by Saturn, Uranus, Neptune, Earth, Venus, Mars, Mercury, and finally, tiny Pluto (the largest of the dwarf planets). Jupiter is so big that all the other planets could fit inside it.

The planets do not have light of their own. They appear brighter when light from the sun falls on them. The surface of the planet reflects the sunlight due to which the planet shines.

UNIVERSE

Natural satellites

An object which revolves round a planet (as the moon revolves around the Earth) is called a **satellite**. The word comes from the Latin word 'satellites', meaning 'attendant'. All satellites move round their parent planets in paths called **orbits**. Seven out of the nine planets in the solar system have satellites or moons. The only two planets which do not have satellites or moon are Mercury and Venus. The Earth has only one moon. The moon of the Earth completes one revolution around the Earth is 27.3 days. It also takes 27.3 days to complete on rotation on its axis. The moon is much smaller than the Earth.

Comets

These are heavenly objects which revolve round the sun like planets but have a very long period of revolution. A comet has a distinct head and a glowing tail which is always directed away from the sun. It brightens as it approaches the sun. Once in many years one happens to see a comet with the naked eye.

Astonishing fact

The sun travels around the galaxy once every 200 million years—a journey of 100,000 light years.

Parts of the Universe

Astonishing fact
Did you know that if you fell into a black hole, you would stretch like spaghetti!

Meteors and meteorites

Meteors are small heavenly objects moving round the sun. Sometimes, they get displaced from their orbit and enter the Earth's atmosphere from outer space with a very high speed. Friction between these objects and atmospheric air causes the objects to get red hot and finally burn out. Meteors are seen as bright streaks of light in the sky. They are therefore called **shooting stars**.

Sometimes, meteors of greater size reach the Earth without getting burnt. Then these are called **meteorites**. Some of the meteorites can be seen in museums.

Asteroids

Asteroids are small heavenly bodies that lie between the orbits of Mars and Jupiter. These are much smaller than a planet and orbit round the sun.

UNIVERSE

Astonishing fact
The nearest galaxy to Earth is Sagittarius Dwarf. It was discovered in 1954 with a distance of 82 light years away followed by Large Magellanic Cloud.

Stars

Each **star** in the sky is an enormous glowing ball of gas. Our sun is a medium-sized star. Stars can live for billions of years. A star is born when an enormous cloud of hydrogen gas collapses until it is hot enough to burn nuclear fuel (producing tremendous amounts heat and radiation). As the nuclear fuel runs out (in about 5 billion years), the star expands and the core contracts, becoming a giant star which eventually explodes and turns into a dim, cool object (a black dwarf, neutron star or black hole, depending on its initial mass). The largest stars have the shortest life span (still billions of years); more massive stars burn hotter and faster than their smaller counterparts (like the sun).

Stars twinkle due to air currents in the atmosphere. The colour of any star depends upon its temperature. They appear to be near each other, but actually they are apart by distances of billions of kilometres. These distances are measured in terms of a very big unit of distance called **light year**. Light year is used to measure distances in the Universe. One light year is the distance travelled by light in one year.

Parts of the Universe

Galaxy

A **Galaxy** or nebula is any large-scale system of stars, interstellar gas, dust and plasma within the Universe. Galaxies have different shapes and sizes. Our galaxy is called the **Milky Way**. This galaxy is spiral in shape and is wider at the centre. It appears as a huge strip of faintly glowing light from north is south across the sky. The sun and about 20 billion stars are a part of this galaxy. There are around hundred billion galaxies in the Universe. These galaxies are the building blocks of the Universe as atoms are the building units of the all substances.

Astonishing fact

The Milky Way galaxy is whirling rapidly, spinning our sun and all its other stars at around 100 million km per hour!

Constellations

A **constellation** is a group of stars which when seen from Earth, form a pattern. The stars in the sky are divided into 88 constellations.

The brightest constellation is **Crux** (the Southern Cross). The constellation with the greatest number of visible stars in it is **Centaurus** (the Centaur - with 101 stars). The largest constellation is **Hydra** (The Water Snake) which extends over 3.158 per cent of the sky.

15

UNIVERSE

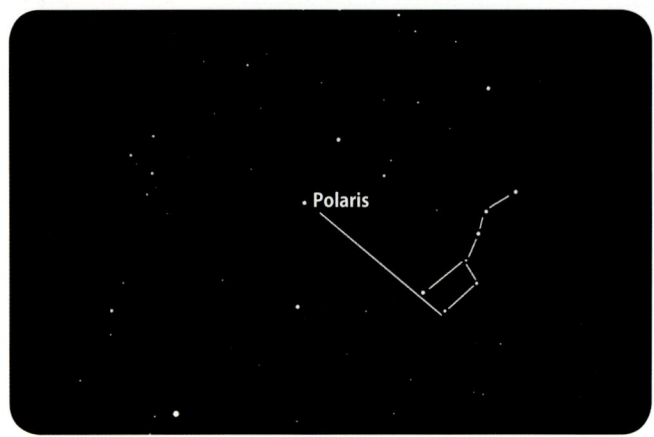

Pole Star

This is a star which is seen directly above the North Pole on the axis of rotation of the Earth. The term 'the Pole Star' usually refers to Polaris, which is the current northern pole star, also known as the **North Star**. It remains stationary at the same place in the north. It is not too bright and has no other star around it. All constellations appear to revolve around the Pole Star. The Pole star lies on the imaginary line joining the two stars, at the end of Ursa Major in the North direction. In ancient times, the Pole Star was used for navigation by the sailors at sea.

Artificial satellites

Artificial satellites are man-made vehicles launched by rockets into the orbit around the Earth. All the artificial satellites have a finite life and will eventually burn like meteors. Artificial satellites have a number of uses or functions. They maybe weather satellites, communication satellites or those which provide information about Earth's resources, etc. While the weather satellites help in forecasting weather conditions and provide warning of cyclones, communication satellites relay telephone and television signals, allowing live transmission of events from all parts of the world.

These artificial satellites can be observed as bright stars, travelling across the sky either just after sunset of before sunrise.

The distance of the planets (from the Earth) is measured by bouncing radar signals off them and timing how long the signals take to get there and back.

Black Holes, Pulsars and Quasars

Black Holes

A **black hole** is a region in space where gravitational force is so strong that nothing can escape from it. A black hole is invisible because it even traps light. The fundamental descriptions of black holes are based on equations in the theory of general relativity developed by the German-born physicist, Albert Einstein.

The gravitational force is strong near a black hole because all the black hole's matter is concentrated at a single point in its centre. Physicists call this point a singularity. It is believed to be much smaller than an atom's nucleus.

The surface of a black hole is known as the **event horizon**. This is not a normal surface that you could see or touch. At the event horizon, the pull of gravity becomes infinitely strong. Thus, an object can exist there for only an instant as it plunges inward at the speed of light!

Astonishing fact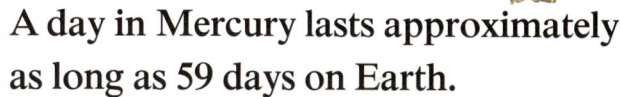

A day in Mercury lasts approximately as long as 59 days on Earth.

UNIVERSE

According to general relativity, a black hole can form when a massive star runs out of nuclear fuel and is crushed by its own gravitational force. While a star burns fuel, it creates an outward push that counters the inward pull of gravity. When no fuel remains, the star can no longer support its own weight. As a result, the core of the star collapses. If the mass of the core is three or more solar masses, the core collapses into a singularity in a fraction of a second.

As they are so small, distant and dark, black holes cannot be directly observed. Yet scientists have confirmed their long-held suspicions that they exist. This is typically done by measuring mass in a region of the sky and looking for areas of large, dark mass.

Many black holes exist in binary star systems. A binary star is a pair of stars that orbit each other. These holes may continually pull mass from their neighboring star, growing the black hole and shrinking the other star, until the black hole is large and the companion star has completely vanished.

The nearest star to us is Proxima Centauri with a distance of 39, 923, 310 million km or 4.22 light years followed by Alpha Centauri at 41, 531, 595 million km or 4.39 light years.

Pulsars

Pulsars are types of neutron stars. A neutron star is the highly compacted core of a dead star, left behind in a supernova explosion. What sets pulsars apart from regular neutron stars is that they are highly magnetized and rotating at enormous speeds. Astronomers detect them by the radio pulses they emit at regular intervals.

A pulsar is formed when a massive star collapses, exhausts its supply of fuel. It blasts out in a giant explosion known as a supernova, the most powerful and violent event in the Universe. Without the opposing force of nuclear fusion to balance it, gravity begins to pull the mass of the star inward until it implodes. In a pulsar, gravity compacts the mass of the star until it forms an object composed primarily of neutrons packed so tightly that they no longer exist as normal matter.

The brightest galaxy in the Universe is Large Magellanic Cloud with a distance of 0.17 million light years from Earth followed by Small Magellanic Cloud with a distance of 0.21 million light years from Earth.

UNIVERSE

Pulsars were discovered in 1967 by Anthony Hewish and Jocelyn Bell at the radio astronomy observatory at Cambridge. Pulsars are found mainly in the Milky Way, within about 500 light-years of the plane of the galaxy. A complete survey of the pulsars in the galaxy is impossible, as weak pulsars can only be detected if they are nearby. Radio surveys have now covered almost the whole sky, and over 300 pulsars have been located.

Pulsars are very strongly magnetised neutron stars, with fields of strength reaching 100 million Tesla (1 million million Gauss, compared with less than 1 Gauss for the Earth's magnetic field).

The rapid rotation therefore makes them powerful electric generators, capable of accelerating charged particles to energies of a thousand million million Volts. These charged particles are, in some way as yet unknown, responsible for the beam of radiation in radio, light, X-rays and gamma rays. Their energy comes from the rotation of the star, which must therefore be slowing down. This slowing down can be detected as a lengthening of the pulse period. Typically a pulsar rotation rate slows down by one part in a million each year: the Crab Pulsar, which is the youngest and most energetic known, slows by one part in two thousand each year.

> Hubble's law showed that Universe is getting bigger and so must have started very small. This led to the idea of Big Bang.

Black Holes, Pulsars and Quasars

Quasars

Many astronomers believe that quasars are the most distant objects detected in the Universe. Quasars give off enormous amounts of energy. They can be a trillion times brighter than the sun! Quasars are believed to produce their energy from massive black holes in the centre of the galaxies in which the quasars are located. Because quasars are so bright, they drown out the light from all the other stars in the same galaxy.

Despite their brightness, due to their great distance from Earth, no quasars can be seen with an unaided eye. Energy from quasars takes billions of years to reach the Earth's atmosphere. For this reason, the study of quasars can provide astronomers with information about the early stages of the Universe.

The word quasar is the short form for 'quasi-stellar radio source'. This name, which means 'star-like emitters of radio waves', was given in the 1960s when quasars were first detected. The name is retained today, even though astronomers now know most quasars are faint radio emitters. In addition to radio waves and visible light, quasars also emit ultraviolet rays, infrared waves, x-rays and gamma-rays. Most quasars are larger than our solar system.

Astonishing fact

During summer in Uranus, the sun does not set for 20 years. In winter, darkness lasts for 20 years. In autumn, the sun rises and sets every 9 hours!

21

UNIVERSE

Astonishing fact

There are about 100 billion galaxies in the Universe. The nearest spiral galaxy to our Milky Way is the Andromeda Galaxy, which is 2.6 million light years away!

Quasars are the most distant objects to ever be detected in the Universe. They also have the largest red shift of any other objects in the cosmos. Astronomers are able to measure speed and distance of far away objects by measuring the spectrum of their light. If the colours of this spectrum are shifted toward the red, this means that the object is moving away from us. The greater the red shift, the farther the object and the faster it is moving. Since quasars have such a high red shift, they are extremely far away and are moving away from us at extremely high speeds. It is believed that some quasars maybe moving away from us at 240,000 km per second or nearly 80 per cent the speed of light.

The first identified quasar was called 3C 273 and was located in the constellation Virgo. It was discovered by T. Matthews and A. Sandage in 1960. It appeared to be associated with a 16th magnitude star like object. Three years later, in 1963, it was noticed that the object had an extremely high red shift. The true nature of this object became apparent when astronomers discovered that the intense energy was being produced in a relatively area. Today, quasars are identified primarily by their red shift. Today more than 2000 quasars have been identified.

Astonishing fact

Ceres is the biggest asteroid in the Solar System – 940 km across and 0.0002 per cent the size of the Earth.

Age of the Universe

The age of the Universe is defined as the largest possible value of proper time integrated along a time like curve from the Earth at the present epoch back to the Big Bang. The time that has elapsed on a hypothetical clock which has existed since the Big Bang and is now here on Earth will depend on the motion of the clock. According to the preceding definition, the age of the Universe is just the largest possible value of time having elapsed on such a clock.

It was estimated to be about 13.7 billion (13.7×10^9) years, with an uncertainty of 200 million years, by NASA's Wilkinson Microwave Anisotropy Probe project (WMAP). However this is based on the assumption that the underlying model that was used is correct. Other methods of estimating the age of the Universe give different ages.

Some recent studies found the carbon-nitrogen-oxygen cycle to be two times slower than previously believed, leading to the conclusion that the Universe must be at least 14.7 billion years old.

The Universe may have neither a centre nor an edge.

Size of the Universe

The size of the Universe is 46 billion light years. This is the distance from planet Earth to the edge of the Universe. 1 light year is equal to 9.46 trillion km. The visible Universe has a diameter of 93 billion light years.

The observable Universe means the edge that light can travel. Remember that we see objects in the Universe because of light. The distance of these objects however, means light takes a long time to travel.

When we look at the Universe, we don't see it as it is, but as it appeared billions of years ago. When looking at faraway galaxies, the light reaching us have been traversing space for billions of years. For this reason, we see the objects and the Universe as it looked billions of years ago.

How does this relate to the size of the Universe? It allows scientists to calculate the dimensions. Scientists determine its size by (among other methods) multiplying the age via the speed of light (299,337 km per second). The age of the Universe is estimated to be 13.7 billion years.

The Virgo Cluster (cluster of galaxies) is 50 million light years away and is made up of 1000 galaxies.

Size of the Universe

Of course, these calculations are limited. It only accounts for the Universe which we can observe. The calculations for the dimension of the Universe go back only as far as light can reach. The rest of the Universe beyond light may well be much bigger.

Some make a distinction between the observable Universe and the actual physical Universe. The observable Universe is the 'edge', the farthest light can travel. Beyond that is the rest of space.

Calculating the size of the Universe can become even more complicated. The measurements don't take into account the expansion of the Universe. Today a lot of scientists believe the Universe is expanding. If that is the case, it means the Universe is getting bigger.

For example, the galaxy that was 2 billion light years away is moving farther away. It means light has to travel much farther to reach Earth. This will affect the calculations of the Universe's dimensions.

Light that travels 13 billion light years doesn't mean the galaxy is 13 billion years distant. With the expanding Universe, it could be much farther.

Astonishing fact

Halley predicted that a comet he had discovered would return in 1758, 16 years after his death, and it really did! It was the first time a comet's arrival had been predicted, and the comet was named after him as Halley's Comet.

Shape of the Universe

There's a continuing discussion among astronomers regarding the actual shape of the Universe. Right now, the most widely accepted model supports that of a flat Universe.

This has been confirmed through accurate measurements made by WMAP (Wilkinson Microwave Anisotropy Probe), a spacecraft that maps out the differences in temperature of the cosmic microwave background radiation (CMBR) across the entire sky. These results, which only have a 2 per cent margin of error, were released in 2008.

Before these seemingly conclusive findings were released, discussions revolved around three possible shapes—flat, closed, and open. To ascertain the actual shape, majority of astronomers were in agreement that they only needed to determine a few significant information about the Universe. One of them was its density.

They knew that if the density was found to be approximately equal to an accepted critical density, then the best prediction would be that of a flat Universe. If it was lower than the accepted value, then the best prediction would favour an open one. Finally if it was higher than the critical density, the prediction would favour a closed Universe.

Evolution of life in the Universe

The Universe began with an unimaginably enormous density and temperature. This immense primordial energy was the cauldron from where all life arose. Elementary particles were created and destroyed by the ultimate particle accelerator in the first moments of the Universe.

There was matter and there was antimatter. When they met, they annihilated each other and created light. Somehow, it seems that there was a tiny fraction more matter than antimatter, so when nature took its course, the Universe was left with some matter, no antimatter, and a tremendous amount of light. Today, there is more than a billion times more light than matter.

About 4.6 per cent of the mass and energy of the Universe is contained in atoms (protons and neutrons). All life is made from a portion of this 4.6 per cent.

> **Planets have magnetic field around them because of the liquid iron in their cores. As the planets rotate, so the iron swirls, generating electric currents that create the magnetic field.**

We are carbon-based life forms. We breathe oxygen. Carbon and oxygen were not created in the Big Bang, but rather much later in stars. All of the carbon and oxygen in all living things are made in the nuclear fusion reactors that we call stars. The early stars were massive and short-lived. They consume their hydrogen, helium and lithium and produce heavier elements. When these stars die with a bang they spread the elements of life, carbon and oxygen, throughout the Universe. New stars condense and new planets form from these heavier elements. The stage is set for life to begin. Understanding when and how these events occur offer another window on the evolution of life in our Universe.

UNIVERSE

Life in the Solar System

Human beings are the only intelligent beings living in our Solar System. There's plenty of excitement, though, about finding micro-organisms elsewhere in our neighbourhood. Recent discoveries on Earth suggest that where there's organic (carbon-based) chemistry, water and an energy source, there's life; no matter what the conditions. As these essentials are commonplace in space, there's a good chance that life is too.

Living organisms have been found alive and well in environments on Earth so apparently hostile that the presence of life on other Solar System bodies seems quite feasible. Mars, the planet that most closely resembles Earth, and Europa, one of Jupiter's moons, both show evidence of water, and so are the focus of plans to look for life.

Did life arise independently on each body? If not, could it have been transferred from one to another? If so, was the common origin a 'seed' planted, perhaps, during collisions with comets, or interstellar dust? Crucial to answering these questions will be greater knowledge about the structure and composition of comets and interstellar dust. Saturn's moon, Titan, also shows promise of revealing the conditions needed for basic organic chemistry to evolve into the chemistry that eventually leads to life.

Astonishing fact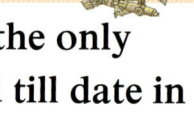

Earth's atmosphere is the only atmosphere discovered till date in which human can breathe.

28

Ultimate fate of the Universe

The ultimate fate of the Universe is a subject of study in the field of cosmology. Either the Universe will exist forever or it will cease to exist at some time. It is unknown which of these possibilities will hold true. It is also not known whether the Universe will continue to support life.

Ever since scientists proved the Big Bang to be the most plausible cosmological theory, and since it only focused more on how it might have all began, their attention started to shift to how the Universe would end. Thus, 4 theories Big Crunch, Big Freeze, Big Rip and Big Bounce have been suggested.

The **Big Crunch** predicts that, after having expanded to its maximum size, the Universe will finally collapse into itself to form the greatest black hole ever.

On the opposite side of the coin, the **Big Freeze** foretells of a Universe that will continue to stretch forever, distributing heat evenly in the process until none is left to be usable enough. Hence, it is also known as the Heat Death.

A more dramatic version of the Big Freeze is the **Big Rip**. In this scenario, the Universe's rate of expansion will increase substantially so that everything in it, down to the smallest atom, will be ripped apart.

Astonishing fact

With powerful telescopes, astronomers can see galaxies 2 billion light years away. This means we see them as they were when the only life forms in Earth were bacteria.

In a cyclic or oscillatory model of the Universe, there will be no end for matter and energy. But for us and the Universe that we know of, there will definitely be a conclusion. In an oscillatory model, the Big Bang and Big Crunch form a pair known as the Big Bounce. Essentially, such a Universe would simply expand and contract (or bounce) forever.

For astronomers to determine what the ultimate fate of the Universe should be, they would need to know certain information. Its density is supposedly one of the most telling.

You see, if its density is found to be less than the critical density, then only a Big Freeze or a Big Rip would be possible. On the other hand, if it is greater than the said critical value, then a Big Crunch or Big Bounce would most likely ensue.

Astonishing fact

The first living creature in space was the dog Laika on board Sputnik 2 in 1957. Sadly, she died when the spacecraft's oxygen supply ran out.

The most accurate measurements on the cosmic microwave background radiation (CMBR), which is also the most persuasive evidence of the Big Bang, shows a Universe having a density virtually equal to the critical density. The measurements also exhibit the characteristics of a flat Universe. Right now, it looks like all gathered data indicating that a Big Crunch or a Big Bounce is highly unlikely to occur.

SETI is the Search for Extraterrestrial Intelligence—the program that analyzes radio signals from space for signs of intelligent life.

Test Your MEMORY

1. What is the Universe?

2. Describe the origin of the Universe.

3. What is the Universe composed of?

4. Describe the parts of the Universe.

5. What is a Black Hole?

6. What is the Solar System?

7. What is the age of the Universe?

8. Describe the size of the Universe.

9. Describe the shape of the Universe.

10. Describe the evolution of life in the Universe.

11. Do you think life exists on any other planet besides Earth?

12. What do you think is the ultimate fate of the Universe?

Index

A
antimatter 5, 27
asteroids 10, 11, 13
atoms 5, 8, 15, 27

B
baryonic matter 8
Big Bang 3, 5, 6, 7, 20, 23, 27, 29, 30
Big Crunch 29, 30
Big Freeze 29, 30
black hole 13, 14, 17, 18, 29

C
Centaurus 15
comets 10, 11, 12, 28
constellation 15, 22

D
dark energy 9
dark matter 9

E
Edwin Hubble 6

G
galaxy 3, 5, 6, 12, 15, 19, 20, 21, 22, 25

H
helium 5, 9, 27
Hydra 15
hydrogen 3, 5, 8, 9, 14, 27

L
light year 14, 18, 19, 20, 22, 24, 29

M
matter 3, 5, 8, 9, 17, 19, 27, 28, 30
meteorites 10, 13
meteors 7, 10, 11, 13, 16
microwaves 7
Milky Way 15, 20, 22
moon 10, 12, 28

N
neutrinos 9
neutrons 5, 8, 19, 27
neutron star 14, 19

O
orbits 11, 12, 13

P
particles 5, 9, 20, 27
planets 9, 10, 11, 12, 16, 27
Pole star 16
protons 5, 8, 27
pulsars 2, 17, 19, 20

Q
quasars 21, 22

R
red shift 6, 22

S
satellite 12
shooting stars 13
solar system 5, 10, 11, 12, 21, 22, 28
spectroscope 3
star 9, 14, 16, 18, 19, 20, 21, 22
sun 9, 10, 11, 12, 13, 14, 15, 21